Caribbean Adventures

GOSPEL ADVENTURES FROM THE CARIBBEAN

Caribbean Adventures

GOSPEL ADVENTURES FROM THE CARIBBEAN

Samuel W Jennings

RITCHIE

John Ritchie Publishing

40 Beansburn, Kilmarnock, Scotland

ISBN-13: 978 1 914273 34 6

Copyright © 2022 by John Ritchie Ltd.
40 Beansburn, Kilmarnock, Scotland

www.ritchiechristianmedia.co.uk

Typeset by John Ritchie Ltd., Kilmarnock
Printed by Bell & Bain Ltd., Glasgow

Foreword

Sam Jennings has just celebrated his ninety-fourth birthday. His has been a very long life – and a very useful one. For decades he has been engaged in preaching the Gospel and giving Bible teaching to believers. He is well respected, greatly valued and much loved.

Back in the 1990s, I heard Sam on several occasions in Bethesda Hall, Linthouse, Glasgow. I was struck by the quantity and quality of his ministry. I still have the notes I took on those occasions. It was well worth making those trips from Fife to hear him! I have also benefitted from reading the books he has written.

I was aware of Sam's visits to the islands of the Caribbean. My friend, Andrew Dawson, of Dollingstown, County Down, Northern Ireland had heard a report that he had given. Sam's account of the places he had visited, the people he had met - and the humorous situations he had encountered! – had been appreciated by Andrew.

How good, then, that Sam has been able to write this book and share his experiences with a wider audience.

In the opening chapter, he describes how salvation came to his family. He writes about his own conversion and then about how he was called to sell his bakery business and enter full-time service. Used by the Lord in his own Northern Ireland, opportunities then opened for him to travel abroad. It is interesting to note that it was a conversation with a sister, Joan Harkness, that led Sam to the United States and that his involvement with the West Indies commenced with the exercise of another sister, Sally McCune.

This book will encourage you. Despite some early opposition to the Gospel, God has blessed, and His work has prospered. You will be introduced to individuals, and indeed assemblies, wholly committed to the Lord, seriously interested in His Word and deeply exercised about sharing the story of salvation with their communities. There is also a great deal of humour!

Sam's visits to the Caribbean were a blessing to those islands. May his record of those visits now be a blessing to all his readers. I commend this book to you.

Fraser A Munro
Windygates
Fife
November 2022

Contents

1 Early Days 9

2 An Opened Door... 19

3 A Missionary Marriage 23

4 Antigua... 33

5 Dominica... 37

6 Barbados 67

7 Further Visits to Barbados............................... 81

8 Helpful Believers... 87

9 Trinidad 117

10 Grenada.. 129

11 Anguilla.. 143

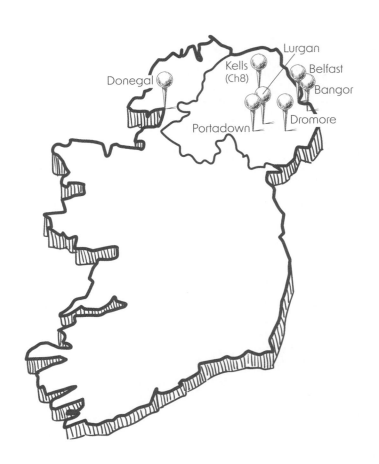

Early Days

About 140 years ago, in the 1880s, there was a well-known pork shop in the town of Portadown in the north of Ireland. It was owned by a gentleman named Rowan Jennings. In those days, this man killed the pigs and did all that was necessary to produce the most delicious pork and bacon. People came from far and near to purchase his goods. His premises were scrupulously clean for the said Jennings had a thing about cleanliness.

This man had three sons: one called Rowan, the oldest, then next came John and the last was Samuel, known as Sam. Rowan turned out to be a keen businessman; he worked with his father in the pork business and later took over the business when his father died. He was one of the few people to own a car in the early days.

John worked at just whatever came along and Sam had three arrows to his bow. He was a trained baker and had a reputation for providing the best of baked goods. He also managed to be trained in a linen factory and was able to maintain linen looms. This skill was called a Tenter in those days. Sam also had the skill of playing the violin. During his youth, he practised up to five hours a day. In the evenings, he taught music and sometimes that was his chief income. Alas, he became an alcoholic; this came about when he joined the navy. He was served rum to start each day and soon became dependent on it. Throughout most of his life the bulk of his earnings were spent on drink.

When the First World War commenced, the three brothers joined the army. They were in the trenches at the forefront of the War. John came through the War without a scratch. Rowan received a bullet near to his heart and the doctors in those days were not sufficiently skilled to remove the bullet in case the heart stopped. Sam was afflicted with gas. This enabled him to get a war pension for the rest of his life. One day, Sam was in a pub and, as usual, played the violin for his drinking companions. One man listened carefully and afterwards said to Sam that he had a daughter who played the organ. Would he come to his house and meet her? Sam did so and met the organist and her sister, Jayne. This sister served him with tea and some cakes. Sam fell for Jayne at once and later married her. They had five children and I was the last of the children born, so Sam Jennings became my father and Jayne became my mother.

Now, salvation through faith in Christ was unknown in my family. None of my uncles or aunts or any other relatives were saved. My mother used to sing in the choir in church, but that was in the past. None of our family were churchgoers.

I was born in Dromore, County Down, Northern Ireland in November 1928. We left Dromore and moved to Portadown when I was six months old, so I remember nothing of Dromore.

I do remember the early days in 5 Tavanaugh Gardens, Portadown.

The street is still there and the house I lived in for a few years is still standing. I went and stood outside the door lately. It was a very wet day and I stood outside remembering the first seven years I spent there.

My father was difficult to live with so my mother left him. She rented a house in Belfast and took the children with her. A month later, my father found out where we were living and one day came and knocked the door. When it was opened, he just walked in. Despite all his drinking and my mother's hardships, they still loved each other and so my Dad remained in the house that was off Tates Avenue, Belfast until the day of his death.

There I lived as a boy and made many friends in the streets where my home was situated. As I have already stated, I was one of five children. I had three sisters and a brother who was called Rowan.

Now, when we were living in Portadown, Rowan had got a job in a foundry in Belfast. He rode a bike to Belfast each Monday and returned home on Friday. During the week he lodged with our Aunt. The sister of my mother, "The organist". There worked beside him a young man who was a Christian. Rowan, my brother, made fun of him and his religion. The young man persevered and kept speaking of Christ the Saviour to him. Eventually the young man saw Rowan saved by the grace of God. This was how salvation first entered into our family.

Now, as I have indicated, Rowan came home to Portadown each weekend. He was ten years older than me and we had wonderful fun together.

When we all moved to Belfast, my brother had only to ride the bike to where he worked. This only took him about fifteen minutes.

I attended an elementary school in Broadway, Belfast, and had a teacher named Mr. Cathcart. Among other things, he took the religious session for a class of young boys, of which I was one.

This man taught us the books of the Bible so we could repeat them. This was a wonderful help to me when the Lord saved me. As for the contents of the Bible, I was totally ignorant. This teacher also preached to us some mornings as well. I remember his words. I was about fourteen at the time. These were his words, "Now, boys, we will read in the book of Revelation. It is easy to find, boys. It is at the back of the Bible, the last book. Nice book this, the Revelation. It tells of people who are going to a place called heaven. There will be no pain, death or crying - just happy people living for ever." Then he raised his voice very fiercely and cried, "This book also tells us of another place called the lake of fire and many will be cast into this place to burn forever and ever - and you could be there."

The boys sniggered at this but I did not. I was scared stiff and feared God and His judgment. In language that I then did not know, I was convicted of sin by the Spirit of God. A few days later, I rode my bike to a little Bible shop that was on the Donegal Road and bought a Bible. This I read each day. I started with the Gospel of Matthew as I knew this began the New Testament. I came to the Sermon on the Mount spoken by the Lord. Now, Chapters 5-7 contain the Sermon on the Mount. I devoured these chapters and sought to live them out day by day. The reason for this is that my mother always said that good kind people would be in heaven. She sang in the choir so she said that she would sing in heaven. I stopped going the cinema; I tried not to take the Lord's Name in cursing, and I tried to be nice to other people. If anyone had asked me for my coat I would have given them my coat and other such like things. However, I totally failed and gave it all up. Then, some weeks later, the words of Mr. Cathcart came home to my mind again, so again I sought to live the commands of Matthew Chapters 5-7. I found this impossible, so went back to my old ways. The fierce words about the burning lake came back to me and I sought to live a good life. Again I failed - and so this went on for two years on and off. I never thought of speaking to my brother Rowan lest he thought me to be a fool. I was totally ignorant of the gospel; I had not even heard the words of John 3:16.

My brother Rowan married a nice girl named Adelaide and they both went into the fellowship of Windsor Gospel Hall. They lived in a small apartment above a shop in Tates Avenue, Belfast. I got a job in a grocer's shop and later started to work in a bakery. This came about because my Dad was working in a bakery owned by George Nichols in Tates Avenue. My Dad cut his hand one day while working and asked me to help him in the bakery. I did so for a week and Mr. Nichols asked me to stay and learn the trade. This was the way I became a baker for the rest of my working days.

I often came to the apartment where my brother lived; running up the stairs two and three steps at a time, I borrowed a little money to go to the cinema. I always paid him back and this went on for a long time. One particular evening, I ran up the stairs into the apartment (or flat as they called such in those days). I found a gentleman sitting in the room as I entered. "Who are you?", he said. I told him and then he asked, "Are you saved?" Now this was the first time I heard the word "saved". I just said, "No!" Then he smiled from ear to ear and said, "It is a great and happy experience to be saved". He looked to be a very happy man indeed. Rowan then came into the room and introduced me to Frank Knox, a gospel preacher who was at that time preaching in Windsor Hall. Mr. Knox then addressed me and asked if I had been to the meetings yet. I answered, "No!" He then invited me to come to the meetings. In my mind I remembered the words of the school teacher and I became afraid that the same fear would overtake me. I made up my mind not to go! Then my brother Rowan asked me to go to the Gospel Meeting and to please him I went one night. The Hall was full of people and I managed to squeeze into the back seat. I do not remember the singing, but Mr. Knox's method of preaching was to take a text and to hammer this home to the mind of listeners. His text that night was that of Ephesians 2: "By grace you are saved by faith and not of works". Time and time again he shouted, "Not by works" - and the message was getting home to my mind. He then shouted the words, "Young man, if you are trying to work your way to heaven, you are working your way to hell and not to heaven". In the first Gospel Meeting I ever attended I heard for the first time that one could never save themselves. My mother was wrong and I was wrong! When I got home from the meeting, I began to think – now how does one get saved if they cannot save themselves? I told Rowan that I would go with him to the meetings again. So I went for about three nights and the gospel of Christ began to enlighten my cloudy mind. I then knew that the Lord Jesus had died for sinners upon the cross. But how to believe or make contact with Christ, I knew not.

One evening, I was sitting reading a book in my own home. One of my sisters was at the mantelpiece, on which stood a mirror, combing her hair, getting ready to go out with her boyfriend. Rowan came in and they talked about the gospel - she also had attended some of the meetings in Windsor Hall. Then Myrtle's boyfriend came and off they went. I was alone with Rowan in the house and I asked him to continue the conversation he had been having with Myrtle. So we talked about salvation. I told him I desired to be saved. He then said that he had prayed for me since he had got saved. I asked him, "How does one connect with Christ? How does one believe?" There was a book sitting on the chair. He took this and said, "Now this is your sin". He then put the book on my knee. He then asked me: "Where is your sin?" I said, "On me!" "Right!" he said. He then took the book and laid it on the armchair, saying, "God took your sins and laid them on Christ - what do you say to that?" I said, "They are on Christ". Rowan then said, "Why not accept that, tell that to God?" Later that evening, I went to some party in a mission hall with some of my friends. My mind was on the words of Rowan the whole evening through. When I got home, I went into my bedroom, got on my knees and thanked God for putting my sins on Christ. I believed that with all my heart and God saved me then and there. I got into bed and soon fell asleep. On awaking the next morning, the first thing that entered my mind was getting saved the night before. I was so happy: all the dread of being lost was gone and I had peace with God. Rowan took me to the meeting that night. On the way home, he said to me, "The meetings will soon be over and you are not saved!" I told him that I had been saved the previous night. We both were filled with joy. We stopped under a street lamp near my home and we both wept for joy.

The news soon got round the Christians in the Windsor Hall that I had got saved. The next night, a lady came to me and told me that she had prayed for me since I first came to the meetings. A big man came and told me the very same. Several young men came to me and said, "You have got saved, big fellow! Well, we young men had a prayer meeting for you each evening after the meeting, praying for your salvation".

So many people told me the same thing. No wonder I got saved, for God answers prayer!

I began to read the Scriptures in earnest, trying to work things out. The beauty and the logic of the Bible amazed me. I went to the Bible Readings at Windsor and also to Donegal Road Hall on Thursday nights. The Hall on Donegal Road had a dozen or so older brethren who were giants in the knowledge of the Scriptures. I began to understand things and drank deeply there of the riches in Christ.

Some of my friends had also got saved in a mission hall in the district; I also went with them to their meetings. The fellowship was good but the teaching was far behind that of Donegal Road and Windsor. Baptism was a little on my mind and one evening I was with my brother Rowan and his wife for tea. One of the overseers of Windsor was also present for the meal. The name of this man was William Jordan. This brother asked me when I was going to get baptised. I told him that this was not too important as lots of Christian were never baptised. He asked me for my Bible that I had with me and also asked Adelaide, Rowan's wife, for a pair of scissors. He then took the scissors to my Bible. I said, "What are you doing?" He explained, "I am going to cut Romans 6 out of your Bible, also Acts 2 and Matthew 28 and Acts 16 and so forth because Samuel does not believe them!" That was enough for me! I got baptised in Windsor Hall shortly afterwards. About a year later, I came into the fellowship and was soon taken by the young men to preach and testify in other halls on Lord's Day evenings.

I met a lovely girl in Windsor Hall called Betsy Kerr. I liked her very much and so asked her out for a walk. She came. Eventually we got married on the 26th July 1954 and had a honeymoon in London.

I worked for a bakery in the town of Lurgan, so we bought a house in Lambeg which was between Lurgan and Belfast. A year later, I bought a bakery in Belfast and so we moved to Belfast. In due course, the bakery did very well and two little girls were added to our family, Sharon and Gillian. We were altogether a very happy family. We then came into the fellowship of Glenburn Hall near to where we lived. I always took an interest in the gospel and full-time preachers. As I had a good standard of living, I had practical fellowship with some workers in Ireland and a few in England as well. Some of the older preachers in Northern Ireland passed on to glory, but the many young men in the assemblies seemed to shun full-time gospel preaching. In a few years about ten of the preachers that I knew passed on to their rewards, but only one man went out full-time to further the gospel. Now all this troubled me and I prayed that the Lord would raise up young men and thrust them forth with the Word of the gospel. This burden continued with me for about three years. Now it was my habit to start work at 6 a.m. and first thing turn up the ovens and stand in the lovely warm atmosphere and pray for a few minutes about the work in Northern Ireland. One morning in doing so, a thought sprang into my mind: why not go myself? Now this thought never left me. Without doubt, it was of the Lord. I told my wife of this and she said that she would be behind me all the way, even to selling her car (we both had good cars) or moving to a smaller house. The Lord spoke to me in several ways, and I was certain that all this was a call to the harvest. I preached the gospel almost every Lord's Day, but I never had the experience of continuing week after week in a series of meetings. I prayed about this and soon the Lord opened the door to a series of gospel meetings in a Belfast hall. The Lord worked and a few souls were saved. This also happened in another assembly in Belfast and an encouraging number were saved by the Lord and went on well. I then informed the leading brethren in Glenburn of my exercise and, after meeting a few times, they commended me to the work of the gospel. They wrote me a very touching letter of commendation. So, I sold my business to one of my older sisters at a giveaway price, to be paid to me by instalments. For the first two weeks, I had no meetings as nobody apart from the Glenburn assembly knew that I had gone out full-time. I spent my time going round neighbours with gospel tracts and spent much time with my Bible. Then I got a phone call from a country assembly to take a Sunday night meeting. The brother who invited me said they would like me for a week of ministry but that would be impossible with my business 80 miles away. I then informed him of my commendation to the work. He was delighted so I had a very happy week in that assembly. Before the week was finished, another assembly nearby invited me for a week of ministry. Then another assembly asked me for a series in the gospel. The brethren in Donegal invited me for meetings and so it went on from then to this present day, 54 years later.

During 1973, I was at a meeting in the country and went for my meal beforehand with a certain couple, Samuel and Joan Harkness. Then Joan said to me, "How would you like to go to America for meetings?" Her brother was there in the Midwest of America and found it impossible to get a preacher for a series in the gospel. I accepted and they sent me my fare. I stayed for about 10 weeks, preaching in many assemblies after the series of meetings I was booked for. This started my travelling experiences which took in Canada, Egypt, Australia, Europe and Scotland and a few times in England - plus, of course, the West Indies, where I made many visits of long duration, which leads to this book!

About my family: my sister Myrtle was saved during a time I preached the gospel in an assembly near to where she lived. I took my father to meetings in Donegal Road and he wonderfully got saved. After my father passed on, my mother lived on her own and I often visited her. One time I called and she told me of a strange dream she had had. This was about three crosses and on the middle one was the Lord Jesus. He called to her and she came up near. She told me His face was covered in blood and He said to her, "This is for you!"

I told her that I had tried to tell her this many times, but that she had always answered by saying that her good works were enough. I was taking meetings in a portable hall near where she lived and she came to the meeting the next night. It happened that I preached on the rapture, the coming of the Lord. On the way out, my mother held my hand and informed me that when the Lord comes, she would rise to meet Him. The Lord used a dream to teach her the gospel. So, like Job 33, "God speaketh once, yea twice, yet man perceiveth it not. In a dream, in a vision of the night, when deep sleep falleth upon men, in slumberings upon the bed; Then he openeth the ears of men, and sealeth their instruction". God's ways are past finding out!

An Opened Door

Yearly conferences have been a big attraction to the believers in the assemblies in Northern Ireland, especially in the country districts. These are mostly in the spring and summer of the year and they have always been very well attended, numbering about 150 in the smallest and up to 400 and more in others. The ministry is generally good and profitable, covering the Biblical themes of exhortation and comfort and doctrine. Often some missionary reports would be included. People enjoy the fellowship with one another after the conferences and gather in little groups known to each other to chatter about the conference, farms, the price of cattle and such things. Sometimes it will be a good half hour or more before all decide to go home. Many are then invited to the homes of believers for an excellent supper.

It was at one of these meetings that I had the experience that led me to visit the West Indies. It took place in the Gospel Hall at Ardmore, near the town of Lurgan. I will never forget how this happened. The time was late April 1980. At a conference in this hall I spoke a little word as did other dear brethren. At the end of the conference the usual refreshment time came and as I was eating of the goodies and chatting to some of the brethren, a little lady approached and talked with me. The conversation opened with her saying: "I could take you to an island where young men would give their right arm to hear ministry like this". Now I must say that my speaking was not mighty or intellectual. I only spoke on what I thought was needed for that time and place. I knew the

19

Ebenezer Gospel Hall Conference, Bridgetown in Barbados

identity of this dear sister, namely Mrs. McCune who laboured in the island of Dominica, one of the windward islands of the West Indies. Without any more words she said, "When can you come to Dominica?" She did not say, "Would you come?" Nor did she say, "Perhaps you could come". Rather, she put it like this: *"When can you come?"* Immediately, I thought to myself: why not? I would like to go! However, I was booked for quite a few meetings for gospel and ministry, so I explained that I would be free for two weeks in May. In informing her of this, she replied "Good, I will be in touch".

With other things in my mind, I thought little more of this conversation until a few days later when I received a letter from Sally McCune with the air tickets – Belfast to London, then to Antigua, then to Dominica. The date on the tickets was for less than a week ahead. The return ticket was after eleven weeks' sojourn in Dominica! All this was paid by the lady herself. What could I do but go? Such a time I had, setting things in order, looking out suitable clothes and cancelling meetings ahead. These cancellations caused patience with some and alarm with others, as well as rebuke and so forth. I explained that the whole arrangement had been taken out of my hands and most were satisfied to arrange the meetings sometime later when I returned.

Now anyone who knew Sally McCune would understand that this was the way she went about things. Something came into her mind and she then went about to see that this was done. She would not cease until the end of the matter. She was a very determined sister in Christ.

When I returned home from that meeting at Ardmore, I never mentioned the subject to my wife. The conversation with the missionary lady was soon forgotten. However, when the tickets arrived, I then informed Betsy of the conversation I had had with Mrs. McCune. Now, as I have already indicated, Betsy was very much behind me in the service of the Lord Jesus. When I was commended to the work, she had stated that she would live in a hut and sell all she had to continue the work for the Lord of lords. On hearing of this conversation and the arrival of the tickets, she stated she would take care of home and our two children all the time I was away. So with my wife in full support of my missionary journey and with the tickets in my hand, I was ready to set out for the West Indies, to the island of Dominica.

A Missionary Marriage

Sally McCune

What I write here was told me by Sally McCune herself when we had supper together one particular evening when I was in Barbados. She told me that this information was known only to a few believers. In writing of this I must take up two stories of two individuals then bring them both together.

Sam McCune was a builder in a time when things were becoming more normal after World War 2. The building trade was booming and Sam was prospering. He was building almost night and day and doing well moneywise. The details of how he became exercised and later called by the Lord to serve in the West Indies are unknown to me. However, I heard him one time giving a report of his labours and in that report he stated that the assembly had been reluctant to commend him on the count that he was doing so well in the building business. They thought that maybe he would later regret the step he had taken. His answer to them was in fact the reverse. He had read to them the call of Peter. He had had the greatest catch of fish in his lifetime, but was called by the Lord to fish for men. He left all and followed the Lord. Sam was doing the same thing: leaving all to follow the Lord in His service in the islands. The leading brethren had no argument against this, so they commended both him and his wife to serve the Lord in the West Indies. He laboured much in a few islands where the gospel was being established and many were blessed with salvation. He was also a wonderful help to young believers, confirming them in their new-found faith in Christ. Again, his knowledge of building was greatly used in the building of halls where a number of believers could meet. This was a most necessary provision in the early days of the gospel. A number of years passed and, sad to say, his dear wife died. Now this formed a problem to him: a man in the West Indies as a missionary without a wife was in a somewhat dangerous position. Attractive women were most abundant in the islands. A man of his standing had to be most careful; a testimony could be questioned at the least display of friendliness to any sister in the Lord. Now this especially applied to the island of Dominica where Sam had a long time exercise to establish the gospel. A man who would serve the Lord in Dominica would of necessity be a married man. So Sam McCune came home to Ireland to find himself a wife from the Lord who would be willing to serve with him, especially in the lovely untouched island of Dominica.

Sally, home in Ireland, was a very well-trained and capable nurse. In fact, she was a teaching nurse. She was saved in a Presbyterian church. She became a very keen Christian. However, she fought against baptism in water by immersion. To her, this was totally unnecessary since she had been sprinkled as a child. Some of her friends sought to convince her otherwise. However, she was determined to have nothing to do with the "strange teaching". Those who sought to set her right gave up the struggle. But, on reading her Bible, Sally was taught by the Lord concerning baptism by immersion. She came to understand that baptism is a symbol of the death and resurrection of the Lord Jesus. Like Paul in Acts 9:18, she arose and was baptised. This all took place in some town in County Londonderry. Later she came to reside in Belfast.

In Belfast, she was exercised concerning where she should gather with other believers. Over a period of time, she learned of the assemblies and after much reading of the Word and searching she came into fellowship among those who sought to gather and to function as the churches in the New Testament. She learned the truth of a local church, the assembly. She then was swift to obey the Lord. I think that the assembly she met with was the one in Ballyhackamore in Belfast. In due time a man surnamed Dillon was attracted to her. She became his girlfriend. He was a well-taught brother with an excellent testimony. After some time they were married and met with the saints in Ballyhackamore which was a large assembly in those days. They were very happy together, but, alas, not for long. After about two years of married life, her husband took a severe heart attack and in a few days he passed away. Sally blamed herself for a long time. Why did she, a trained nurse, see no symptoms of heart trouble? Apparently, there had been no symptoms. After a time she was convinced the will of the Lord had been done.

In this state she continued her working life as a nurse and her spiritual home remained Ballyhackamore Gospel Hall. Unknown to her, Mr. Sam McCune had made this his assembly home when on furlough.

In due time brother Sam McCune came home on furlough. Actually, he had it in mind to seek a sister who would meet his requirements and become his wife. One Sunday morning before the meeting started, Mrs. Sally Dillon came into the hall. She took her seat with others, all there to remember the Lord. Brother Sam watched her walking in, it would seem, and observed her when she took her seat. A few days later, after finding out who this lady was, he made up his mind. Later in that same week, he phoned her and asked her out to dinner! At once she refused, saying that she was a one man woman and had no interest whatever in another husband. The like of this she never desired or dreamed of! She was content to remain a widow the rest of her life. Then Sam McCune told her it was a sort of Christian arrangement he had in mind to enable him in missionary work and at this Sally consented to go out with him for dinner.

A few days later, he arrived in his car to take her out for a meal. He had arranged a booking in a good hotel somewhere in the country. They had a nice meal together and a warm chat concerning many topics. She was no doubt wondering what this was all about! In fact, he was searching her character for suitability for what he had in mind.

At last, Sally said, "Now what is this business or arrangement you have in mind?" Sam told her of his mission work and his desire to bring the gospel to the shores of Dominica. He explained that a man could not do this alone. It would be necessary for a man and wife together to do this evangelising. Then he proposed to her. She said, "I would need some time to think about this". He answered, "Take as long as you like but I intend to go back to the islands in a month or so". Then Sally immediately said, "Alright, I am willing to be your wife and to accompany you to the islands where you think the Lord would indicate". Very few women would make a quick decision like this. The way things turned out it was evident all was of the Lord. Sally informed me she took all this to be the will of God for her. She was a very earnest believer and sought always to glorify the Lord in her life.

After a little while, they were married and Sally became Sally McCune. After a few days, they set off for Bermuda where Sam had been working before he came home. There were a few assemblies on the island and Sam was seeking to strengthen them and to help with the gospel as much as was in him. Sally got a job as a nurse in the local hospital and sought to help with the gospel in any way she could. After a year or two there, Sam decided it was time to move to Dominica and see about the planting of the gospel in that untouched island. I will seek to write more about this island later in this book. Suffice to say, the population was about 73,000. Most lived together without marriage and all was ruled and totally given over to the Roman Catholic Church. Many priests lived on the island at that time, serving their church with great vigour, hence there was much opposition to the new missionaries and the gospel they sought to preach. The task turned out to be most difficult and discouraging, but this man and wife served long hours each day with great faith that the Lord would work in due course - and so He did.

Sally told me of those hard days, when they went through a village with tracts and sought to talk to the people. They had found the people most friendly, but at the end of the day, the priest had come and had handed them a bucket full of their torn up tracts. He had followed them to undo all they sought to do. At least, they got a free bucket! While in this service from day to day something became evident. Sally was able to outwork her husband Sam. He had to rest and finally stop for the day. Sally, however, carried on until darkness fell upon the village. She turned out to be a born missionary. Nothing daunted her, and on she went, facing all difficulties and trusting the Lord to care for the seed of the gospel.

By and by they saw a few people saved in a few villages of the island. Then they had the task of helping them in their happy faith in Christ. Dominicans are generally a very happy people in spite of poverty. They learn to make do and also to make little go a long way. However, when they get saved, they are happier to a greater degree: salvation to them is so fresh and wonderful. A difficulty stood in the way of this spiritual education, as many of the young men, like others on the island, had never learned to read. Sally McCune took it upon herself to teach the promising young men to read. In one village the work went forward in a spiritual way and enough had trusted Christ to form an assembly. The place was called Salisbury. From where did this name come? Dominica had the misfortune as other islands in the Caribbean to suffer from invasion and to be then controlled by other world powers. Dominica had changed hands to the French, then to the Spanish, then to the British, then back to the Spanish. Each of these countries gave names to places on the island. The result is that some villages and towns have French names, others Spanish and some others have English names. Roseau is the capital. There is a Petite Savanne. There are many places with English names, hence the place where the first assembly was planted was named Salisbury.

Mr. McCune, being of the building trade, built a hall for the believers. The newly saved brethren helped as some of them had some skills in building. In fact, one of the new believers was a builder by trade. He had a little ongoing business and his name was Frederick. His wife also got saved and they set up a lovely Christian home in the midst of much darkness. A few believers were in other places or villages. They were not as yet well enough developed to form assemblies, but within a few years assemblies were established.

Mr. and Mrs. McCune were kept busy. They were teaching the believers to read their Bibles and teaching them the basic truths. There were these building projects as well as attempts to spread the gospel. After almost six years they felt they could leave the work to have a short well-earned furlough. So they set off for Ireland and home. Sam McCune went about a few assemblies in Northern Ireland giving missionary reports. Both he and Sally were revived in health somewhat and had a wonderful rest. After a short time, they set out to return to Dominica. They split their journey to stop with some friends in Bedford, England, for two nights before setting off to the London airport and thence to Dominica. Sadly, the day before they were to set off, Sam McCune's spirit left his body and went to be with the Lord. He was called home as we say. Now this was terrible for the friends who had lovingly given the hospitality and more so to Sally herself. She took things in hand very bravely and got the body home to Northern Ireland. This took a lot of time and trouble. After the funeral in Ballywalter, the place of his burial, the believers thought this would be the end of Sally McCune as a missionary. However, they were mistaken! About two days after the funeral, Sally McCune was on the flight back to Dominica. With the one assembly formed and a few scattered believers, Sally McCune laboured for twelve years. During that time, she established meetings for children in many places. These were very well attended for children abound all over the island. On top of this, she was helping some womenfolk who had got saved and who needed help in understanding the Bible.

Some of the dear younger brethren began to take an interest in preaching. This helped wonderfully in getting the gospel out to others. Two little halls were built by these brethren in fruitful areas and they sought from time to time to have a few weeks of gospel meetings. The Lord blessed this work and a few got saved. Sally sent reports home to Northern Ireland and also to Canada and the States. Canadian brethren took a great interest in the work in Dominica and eventually the Lord exercised a brother named Peter Simms from British Colombia to go to Dominica and to preach the gospel. The outcome of this was that he and his wife and family were commended by the assemblies to Dominica.

Peter and his family were able to find and rent a house in due course and he commenced his service for the Lord and His people. Some time after, another brother called Ken Taylor, also from Canada, joined in the work in Dominica. Later, in my first visit to this lovely island I met Peter and shared with him in the gospel. More about that later! In due course a little assembly was planted in Roseau the capital. I would have called it a little town!

There were people dwelling in little huts on one side and some more well-to-do people living in fine houses on the other side. However, an assembly was planted there, meeting in some place, maybe rented. Later on, the assemblies in Canada were exercised about building a hall in Roseau to house the assembly that met there. A fine hall was built, including toilets etc. A very spacious and furnished apartment with two bedrooms was also added to the back of the hall and Sally McCune had this granted to her as she needed it. Later, when Ken Taylor arrived Sally let them have the apartment for his wife and children and she rented a house for herself about half a mile from the hall. The work went forward and another assembly was planted and so on. The many meeting places for children that Sally had started and managed became useful in contacts with children and parents when the gospel was preached. The two or three little buildings that the Dominican brethren built were also greatly used. Peter also got engaged in prison work; that was not by any means easy. The prison premises were primitive; many of the inmates were imprisoned for murder and were serving long sentences. The Law was not convenient or easy on the criminal in Dominica. Their prison cells were small - simply holes in the rock with strong iron bars enclosing them. I am writing about conditions about forty years ago - I would think that things have changed a lot since then.

Now it was to this island that Mrs. Sally McCune invited me to come. She provided the tickets and in a few days returned to the island and awaited my arrival.

Saint John's
Harbour

4 Antigua

The prepaid ticket that I received from Sally McCune was from London to Antigua, then to Dominica a day or two afterwards. There were no direct flights from any major cites to Dominica at that time and I am sure that is still the case today. So I bade farewell to my dear wife and my two girls and set out on my travels to the West Indies. Crossing the Atlantic was nothing new to me; I had travelled to the U.S.A. and Canada on quite a number of occasions. If I remember right, the flight lasted almost ten hours. When the plane began to descend, I looked down upon an Island in the Caribbean for the first time. The water was so clear, one could see deeply into the calm water with patches of seaweed clinging to the bed of the ocean. Then the plane came in low over the land. Trees abounded and little wooden homes with the lights shining out of a multitude of windows. It was now getting dark. The airport consisted of long landing strips to accommodate large planes and there were a few small buildings. The reception area was not as large as we are used to in England and Belfast. The plane was very large with every seat taken. On arrival many people came out of the plane and headed for the arrival door. Most of the people were on holiday, I expect. The staff were most efficient and soon I was through Customs. I had no difficulty in finding my contact. It was arranged that a brother, a native of Antigua, would meet me. I saw this dear man standing with a large card held forth with my name written on it. I met him and said, "So you are brother Dalmer Edwards". "Yes, and you are brother Jennings", he replied. He gave me a large hug in his lovely brown arms. He carried my baggage and in a little aged car drove me to his house where I was to stay a day or two. This was my first taste of the islands of the Caribbean. Once out of the plane I could feel the heat, quite warm but not unbearable. So different from my home town in Northern Ireland!

Dalmer was Antiguan born as well as born again and had been commended by the local assemblies to the work of the Lord. We soon became good friends and I stayed with him a few times in later years when I was travelling via Antigua to other islands. He had a lovely personality, and it was easy to just love him in the Lord. I think this feeling was mutual. Now Dalmer was used to Irishmen, because Samuel Maze from Belfast had been a missionary there for some time and Sammy had worked closely with him. Also I understand friends from Ireland visited Sammy in Antigua from time to time. The Lord used Sammy richly all the time he laboured in Antigua. Dalmer always had a dream of visiting Ireland, but, as far as I know, that dream was never fulfilled. On arrival at his very neat bungalow, I met his wife and daughters. Mrs. Edwards was a most charming lady and a qualified nurse in the local hospital. Their two daughters were bright smiling girls and nicely dressed in bright clothing. They were, however, a little shy at having an Irishman in their home. After a night's sleep and a good breakfast, Dalmer took me for a trip round the island in his ancient car. The scenery was beautiful, so no wonder so many people come to holiday there. Many lovely sandy beaches surrounded the coastline and St. John's harbour was a sight I will never forget. From a hill we looked down on the very large harbour of St. John's and saw that it was full of anchored yachts that looked to be very expensive. We had a lunch in a nice place and after a few hours of taking in the brightness and the beauty of the island, we headed for home for a siesta. A few years later during another visit to Dominica, Dalmer paid me a visit. We had a few meetings together and it was wonderful to have his company. I laughed at his exercises every morning, lifting arms and legs and throwing them all over the place. I missed him so much when the time came for him to travel home to Antigua.

In the evening, a meeting was arranged for me to give a word of ministry. Now there were two assemblies in the island at that time and both were represented at the meeting. The believers seemed to be happy indeed, with so many smiling faces to welcome me. Now this was mild in comparison to believers I met on the other islands in later days. However, it was a lovely welcome to the Island of Antigua. The company numbered about fifty and we had a profitable time of fellowship and teaching. All were so sorry I was not staying on the island for a longer period. The next day Dalmar took me to the airport and I headed for Dominica. Dalmar was sorry to see me go, and I felt it also leaving him. I hoped that I would get on as well with all the other brethren I would meet in Dominica.

This turned out to be the first flight of many that I made with LIAT, the flying company of the West Indies.

The islanders made fun of the company, saying it was well named: Luggage Left in Any Terminal! The planes were small with generally just one pilot: he just sat at the controls with nothing between him and the passengers. Now, at last, I was on the way to Dominica.

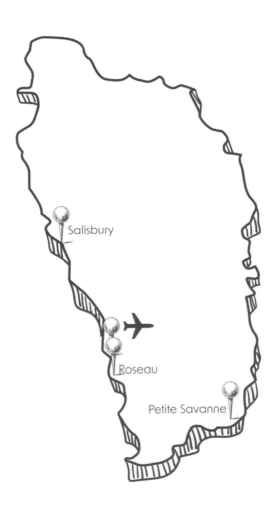

Dominica

The landing of planes in Dominica was legendary and most difficult for the pilots. The company at that time kept the same pilots on this flight because of the benefit of long experience. The landing strip in Roseau was not too long because level places were not in abundance on the island. The small strip was surrounded by high mountains, so the pilots had to approach from the sea and just in time swing round to approach the landing strip. Strong winds from around the mountains made this most difficult, hence the skill required in landing a plane. For the first time ever, I really felt frightened on a plane and I had flown many flights in the past. However, the pilot, and I was just behind him, was as calm as could be and after a few turns we landed safely.

On coming off the plane with the other nine passengers, the first thing we all encountered was the overwhelming company of mosquitoes that greeted our arrival. I had experienced mosquitoes somewhat in Antigua but nothing like this. To most people arriving on Dominica this was a great problem. I remember once meeting an American missionary from another island a year or two later. He visited Dominica and sent home a report that the mosquitoes were so large, that if you could catch one, you could pluck off the head and three legs and use it as a stool to sit on to milk the cows! The said missionary was not connected with the assemblies but with some Christian society in the States. The bites resulted in very irritating lumps and often they became quite serious. Some folk were immune to the bites but, alas, I was not one of them.

I learnt later by experience that the mosquitoes were very crafty; generally they bite one from behind - the back of the arms rather than the front, and the same with the legs, especially the ankles. They nearly overcame me at one stage and I suffered a lot until I developed some immunity to them. In later times when I got a bite, I was itchy for about 5-10 minutes and that was it. A few years later when I brought my wife, Betsy, with me to the islands they made havoc of her from the moment of her arrival.

Going through customs and immigration in Dominica took quite a long time for only ten passengers. We stood in a row in a little run-down hut or shed and a little over half an hour later we were all through at last. During this time, the heat was unbearable in the small hut. There was little ventilation. I thought I was a spy from some place in Europe or a member of the Mafia from the questions I was asked. I answered that I was a Christian on a sort of holiday but intended to teach the Bible among the few Christians on the island. I think all the questions were unnecessary; it really was just to take up the time of the people who worked there. I am sure all things are different now. At last, when I came out of the hut, Mrs. McCune was waiting to meet me with a dear brother I knew so well, Ron Cunningham, a missionary from a country that had changed its name to Tanzania. Why was he there? I did not know but he had been on the island for about two months. Sally never told me this. This was just like her - you knew of something when she was ready to tell you. Sally kept many things to herself and only expressed them when it was necessary. When I met Ron, it was a mutual pleasure. We embraced each other with Christian love. I had known Ron for many years even before the time he left Ireland as a missionary to Africa. He was glad of the company because he was lonely and I was glad of the fellowship of one who could explain to me many things that I needed to learn about the island and the saints there. Ron had an exercise to visit Dominica after Hurricane David swept the island, leaving terrible damage in its wake. The local people had spent many months working, endeavouring to get things back to normal.

A few remarks about Hurricane David are now needed. In September 1979, this hurricane at first was on a course for Barbados. If it had arrived there, Barbados would have been almost completely destroyed. The island was quite flat - only about 300 feet above sea level - so the damage would have been terrible. When the hurricane was heading for Barbados, the people of Barbados prayed earnestly, both Christian and non-Christian. The winds then changed direction and headed for Dominica and the Dominican Republic. In all, the death toll was 1500 souls and thirty-seven of these were from the people of Dominica. The people of Dominica had been informed that the storm was not coming in their direction, so any preparation for the storm had been minimal. Then the course changed and in a few hours the hurricane hit Dominica. The rain was horrendous and the waves higher than a two-storey house. Now, Dominica is very mountainous and the water reached up the hills and then rushed down again. It was this that did most of the damage. Houses were just swept down and carried out into the sea. 60,000 people had damage to their homes and many houses were lost altogether. Cars were lifted into the air and flung to the ground a long way off. Cows and other animals were blown away and never seen again. The winds reached 150 miles per hour.

At that time, Ron was home in Ireland for a furlough. On hearing the news of this devastation in Dominica, he felt exercised to go and help. He left his wife at home and travelled to the island to help the believers as well as he could - and this he did.

A brother told me that the little lady next door to him went out to look and he warned her to get inside. She hesitated and, lo, the wind caught her and she was carried up into the sky. Then a strange thing happened - the wind was whirling around beneath her and she started to descend. It lowered her to the earth, right beside her door, and she ran into the house and slammed the door!

By and by, Ron came to know quite a lot of the brethren and the great need that existed there. The hall in Roseau that was built with much help from Canada suffered some damage to the roof. It was repaired shortly afterwards. The people of Dominica after that referred to buildings and suchlike as A.D. = "After David" or B.D. = "Before David". One interesting thing: Britain had donated a new school bus for the children of the island. It had only been used about two days and the driver in the evening parked the new bus under a huge tree to shelter from the sun. This is what people did with cars in Dominica and other islands. That night the hurricane hit and that huge tree was uprooted and the trunk fell right across the bus. Someone who witnessed this said that he saw the wheels shoot off and fly away and that the noise of the bus being crunched was frightening. The bus was flattened to about three feet from the ground and I saw this a few days after I arrived. Today, a part of the tree is still there and underneath is the bus rusting away. It is one of the sights in Dominica!

Sally then brought us home to the apartment that was behind the hall. She would not let us stay in the house while she was there. "A bad testimony", she would say. The hall was built in the Canadian style with a basement. So the toilets and the room and kitchen were all under the ground level. That is where Ron and I slept.

Alas, the kitchen had a stove but no gas and the cupboards were empty. There was not a dish, spoon or knife. The kitchen was never used. Then there was the room for guests. Ron and I were the first such guests. The room was about 12 feet square and contained two single beds that Ron made when he arrived in Dominica. The beds were very well made, I must say. A framework of wood like a table with four legs. On top was a thin foam mattress that can be bought on the island. I do not think there were any spring mattresses on the island at that time. Again, there was a small table for use of study, and a few other items. All was very primitive but they served the purpose. Ron had the beds in the middle of the floor instead of up against the wall that contained the two louvered windows that were level with the ground outside the hall. I thought it strange that the beds were in the middle. It sort of depleted the space. However, Ron was very wise. He informed me that large ground crabs were roaming about the gardens of Dominica. These were peculiar to Dominica – they were not found on any of the other islands of the Caribbean. The next day I saw these crabs for myself. They were about the breadth of a hand and they moved very quickly indeed. Ron was afraid of a crab coming in through the window because of the ground level and falling upon the sleepers if the beds were against the wall. The window, of course, had to be opened at night to provide a current of air over against the warm nights of the island. In fact, a few years later a brother from Canada paid a visit to Peter Simms and stayed in the little apartment. He pushed the bed over against the wall beneath a window to get more air. He must have thought it to be a silly place for a bed, the middle of the room. However, he soon saw the reason. In the night he felt something on his face. He put his hand on his head in the dark and, of course, he touched a large crab which immediately pushed its claws into his head. The brother jumped up and ran around in the dark looking for the light switch. His shouts raised the whole neighbourhood, they tell me. Many gathered in the streets wondering who was getting murdered. Therefore, brother Ron was very wise indeed, but then he was used to jungle conditions. Sally McCune had named this apartment the "Prophet's Chamber". Ron had a working knowledge of the Dominican brethren who formed the assemblies at that time.

My first day began with Sally and Ron showing me around Roseau in her old car. I was also taken to some of the villages around the coast a little bit. I thought it was all so beautiful and unspoilt. No telegraph poles or advertising hoarding etc. I think at this point I must give a little description of the Island of Dominica.

The island was about 39 miles north to south and about 16 miles east to west. Mountains were everywhere; all the villages around the coast were built on steep hills. The mountains were covered

View from the Land Side of Roseau in Dominica

with greenery: trees, bushes and other things grew in abundance. The growth was so thick it was impossible to walk or climb the hills without something to cut and clear a path; to do otherwise would be a defeating task. Very few villages were to be found in the mountains and the few that existed had a very narrow road leading down to the coast. Water was abundant. I was told that there were over three hundred rivers on the island. Some of these were just babbling brooks, others were raging torrents. In the middle of the island was a rain forest. In fact, all the time I was there it rained most days and very heavy showers at that. I often think of the nights I slept in the prophet's chamber, being kept awake by the rain rattling on the tin roof of the hall. Even in the basement I could hear the rain.

As well as an impenetrable forest, there lived quite a few wild boars. Scattered all over the forests, they often came out onto the roads in front of cars. Dominica is the only island in the Caribbean that had snakes. I am glad to say that the snakes were not poisonous and I never saw any on my travels. As for insects, they were everywhere, especially when the darkness began to fall. Some of these insects were quite large as the cockroach, the length of a finger and the wings terribly sticky. I often looked at the unspoilt beauty of Dominica and praised the Lord of creation. As Ecclesiastes 3 verse II puts it: "He hath made everything beautiful in his time". Most of the little dwellings were built on ground that was levelled first before building, but some had one side of the house propped up on stilts. Few houses had the luxury of bathrooms and kitchens and most were without running water. The women cooked outside in the garden and the children carried water when needed from the nearest river. They could walk quite fast with a large pail, filled to an inch from the top, on their heads without spilling a drop. The roads were in very poor condition, dusty with large potholes everywhere. Driving a car was a slow process. One seldom if ever got into the higher gears in any kind of car. Journeys took a long time. An example of this is a drive from Roseau to Petite Savanne; it took about three hours to complete the twelve miles. The people were very poor yet very happy. Smiling faces were everywhere. I found it easy to love the people and appreciated them more and more as I lived on their island. Children were everywhere, playing on the streets without fear with the most primitive of toys such as hoops made from bicycle wheels and skipping ropes. Most people lived off the land and sold their produce in the markets. The men did the work and the women did the selling. Bananas grew by the millions both in the gardens of people and in the wilds of the mountains. Oranges also grew wild, even by the side of the roads. They fell in abundance to lie on the ground and were just left to rot there. The oranges were very green so there was no market for them; however, they were filled with delicious juice. I remember a brother brought me a large box which contained about forty oranges. I thought they would rot before I ate them all. However, I found I could make a nice drink by cutting them and squeezing out the juice. About three oranges filled a glass. I had no trouble using all the oranges. Another brother asked me if I would like a few bananas. I said that I would and the next day he appeared with a whole stock of bananas. Now these did go bad before I could eat them all. Very few of the people were married; rather they lived with partners. This was the way of life there at that time. It has, sadly, become the way of this perishing world. After eleven weeks living on the islands of the Caribbean, when I came home, everything seemed grey and dull. I missed the sunshine and the hills as well as the people.

As to the assemblies and the believers, brotherly love was really experienced. They were first generation Christians and most, if not all, were eager to learn of their Lord Jesus and to know His Word. I had never come across such a hunger for the Word in all my experience. My first ministry meeting was in Roseau and the attendance was around fifty or sixty each night. The notebooks were out in abundance and the pencils and pens writing as fast as they could, among those who could write. So many of the believers could neither read nor write. This is not the case today. Education is free and of a good standard to all children. I saw great improvement the next time I visited Dominica about a year later. One of the brethren was a school teacher and he turned out to be a pioneer in the education of the islanders. Back to the notes, many of the saints did not need notes as most of the brethren and some sisters as well had the most wonderful memories. I found later that a brother would listen to you preaching the gospel and the next night he would be in another hall preaching your same message almost word for word.

I took to the young brethren right away and they took to me. I had wonderful times with Ron going round the halls that were not too far from Roseau. I preached short messages but sought to present Scripture in all its beauty. Ron preached long messages and the people never got restless when the meeting went very much over the time.

I remember one night after the meeting Sally asked Ron to drive a dear brother to his home in the hills about 7 miles distant. He had walked to the meeting! I went with Ron. On the way home, the car stopped. We were in the middle of hills on a narrow road - and in the darkness as well. We both sat on the ground, backs leaning against the front wheel, looking at the stars in the very warm evening. We thought Sally would miss us and send some brother to look for us. After almost two hours another car passed and stopped. A man stepped out of his car to help us. We had stopped half-way up a very steep hill. He suggested turning the car round so that it would be facing downhill and trying the engine with a good run. We did that with his help and the car started. Again we turned around and set off for home. The man stayed until we got safely on our way. This is typical of the inhabitants of Dominica: always ready to help anyone, black or white. On arrival home, we found that Sally had just gone to bed. She told us the next morning that it was good experience for us. It would help us to trust the Lord in every difficulty!

I always arose in the mornings before seven as it was too warm to stay in bed. Yet it was cool enough to study the Scriptures. I did this each day. Every morning and some afternoons the young men would visit me in the prophet's chamber, just to talk about the Word and assembly life. All the folk worked on the land and the brethren called with me on the way to their piece of land to labour for the day.

I remember in my first few days on the island the mosquitoes had bitten me quite a lot, especially on my ankles. Large blisters had formed on my skin. The blisters were both itchy and painful. I thought that if this got any worse I might have to go home. Ron was well trained in nursing and came to the rescue. He had homeopathic ointment with him and this helped me in a matter of a day or two. One can imagine how I felt when the day came for Ron to return home. We saw him to the plane, embraced with brotherly love and off he went. I watched the plane ride the sky until it was out of sight. How I missed him!

The evenings were long. The meetings were from 6.30pm to 7.30pm or so and I had the whole evening there by myself after a cup of tea with Sally, who then went early to bed. I had a little tape-player with me and some tapes of music. I listened to these time and time again. I also did a lot of reading. Before I got into bed each night I went round the room looking for land crabs. There were always some, as many as 6-10 that had come in through the window during the day. There was a large broom in the unused kitchen that the sisters used to sweep out the hall. I made use of this to slaughter crabs every night. The sisters noticed the broom becoming worn, torn and ragged; I never informed them how this came about! As for showers, there was none in the hall. Toilets and a sink, yes, but not a proper bathroom. This was a luxury in Dominica. However, I found a large jam tin made to contain seven pounds. Every afternoon I filled the sink with water and kept the tap running and scooped the water into the tin and turned it upside down over my head several times. It was cold but refreshing. The toilet was equipped with a water escape in the floor. There was a shower in the apartment but that was for the use of Sally and whoever were living in the apartment. There was hot water in the apartment bathroom but Sally just used the cold tap. She refused to use electric to heat the water. "The Lord's money was not for her comfort but for the work" was her policy.

As to Roseau, there were few restaurants. I only found one, run by a sister from the country. She had been destitute and Mrs. McCune had set her up with a little business in a hut, just about 3 tables. Sometimes I went there and had something to eat. I am a very fervent lover of ice-cream and found it nearly impossible to obtain. Even when I did so, it was a poor example of ice-cream. I was warned by the brethren never to eat mountain chicken because it was made of large frogs' bellies and not with chicken. Large frogs were everywhere in the fields and bushes and people caught them to make mountain chicken. I do not know how they got that title for this particular dish.

I was booked for three nights to speak in the Petite Savanne assembly. Sally took me there in the car and it took us three hours to accomplish a twelve mile trip! The road was horrendous with large potholes so deep that if a wheel rode into one, it was difficult to get the car to move out of it. This called for stopping and starting. Again, the road went up into the mountains and in places narrow hairpin bends confronted a driver, without room to pass another car. The drivers kept their finger on the horn so anyone coming in the opposite direction could know they were coming round the blind bend. We had to do the same. These roads were without a fence of any kind and hundreds of feet down one could see the form of wrecked cars, quite a few. In another place, the road was along the beach which was covered with rocks and stones. There were high cliffs on one side and the sea on the other. If the tide was in, the road was covered and one had to wait a few hours until the waters had receded. At this point, let me mention that donor countries, including Britain, tried to help Dominica. At times they sent them money to repair the roads. That was a great occasion: every able man, and women too, came to earn a few days' pay. They filled up the potholes with sand with a little layer of cement on top. When the rain came - and that was quite frequent - the water rushing down the roads carried sand and all with it. So, the next day they were back to square one! However, everyone was happy. They got two days' pay out of the job and that helped a lot to put food on the table and other things.

So after three hours of gruelling driving, which I did, Sally drove her own way home as I was booked to stay for three nights. Petite Savanne was a nice little village of a few hundred people. Houses were mostly just shacks. Few had bathrooms etc. I stayed with a dear brother and his wife with their three children, all girls as I remember. The home was primitive indeed but they made me most welcome. They felt it was an honour to have me in their home and this they said so sincerely. I had a nice little bedroom with a curtain for a door, a window and a bed and table. I hung my clothes on hooks on one of the walls. One of the girls brought me a pail of water day by day from the river which was about a quarter of a mile away and carried it on her head without spilling a drop. A bathroom was lacking in the house as well as a kitchen. I washed in the mornings from the bucket of water and cleaned my teeth and spit out the window. All the water I washed with ended up going through the window. Outside the window were banana trees covered with toothpaste etc. I think this room belonged to the girls. The wife did the cooking outside on a little stove that sent thick smoke into the air. Amazingly so, the meals were great, plentiful and most tasty.

Now every time I went outside, the girls asked me if I was going to the toilet. I said, "No, just out to get some fresh air". I wondered why they asked me this question every time I went out. However, I was asked the same question by the girls and when I answered, "Yes", they handed me a toilet roll. I said, "Why not keep it outside with the makeshift toilet?" They answered, "It would be stolen". I learnt that toilet paper was a luxury on the island and quite expensive to buy. I am sure that things are different now as progress is found in the most primitive places. The first night after the meeting the bed I was to sleep on was covered with crawling insects. I called the man of the house in to see this and he said, "You kept the window open. These things come in when darkness falls". He informed me that they were harmless. He lifted each with his fingers, crushed them and threw the whole lot out of the window and shut it. The three-night stay was quite different from any I had experienced and I enjoyed the unspoilt quality of it all. The folk did all they could to make my stay a happy one and so it was. Before I came to Petite Savanne, I purchased a box of cornflakes in Roseau. Quite expensive they turned out to be! The first morning at breakfast I took the cornflakes to the table. The little girls just sat looking at me. I said, "Would you like some?" They almost jumped with joy. In fact, the large box of flakes only lasted that morning and the next. When the morning came that I had to leave them, the little girls were almost in tears. They were so sorry to see me leave.

As for the meetings, there were about forty in fellowship and all the brethren were well taught in the Scriptures. They were more advanced than those in other assemblies. They just loved sound Bible ministry.

I think I took up chapters from the book of Judges. I was asked not to consider the time; they were prepared to listen as long as I could speak. We had a wonderful three nights around the Word. After each meeting I was surrounded by eager brethren with their intelligent questions. They also had developed in the ministry and could speak well. They knew the Word and were able to pass it on to others. It was a pleasure to be with them for the three nights. The little time was most heavenly. Joy was in every heart, including my own.

In August 2015, Dominica was hit by Hurricane Erika and terrible damage resulted for the island. Petite Savanne especially took the brunt of the storm. The winds were not as severe as Hurricane David but the rain was horrendous. Older people said they had never witnessed such heavy rain in their lifetime. The rain started mudslides that got stronger and more voluminous as they swept down the hills. Petite Savanne lay in the path of the worst of these and had to be evacuated. However, in spite of this precaution at least twenty-seven people lost their lives. To this day a few damaged houses stand and some folks live in them even though they face danger in the future. The people of Petite Savanne were moved by the government to another locality and houses were provided for many of them. I understand that the assembly in some way is still functioning.

Here as elsewhere, I found that many of the people could not read or write. This was a great hindrance when they got saved. Sally McCune did a great work in teaching many of them to read. Yet, in spite of this obstacle, the saints of Petite Savanne were very able in the Scriptures and prayed most intelligently in the meetings. The time came for my departure. Sally had arrived to take me back to Roseau. The believers all requested me to return as soon as possible. Petite Savanne, I think, was the high water mark in my first visit to Dominica.

A few years later, I paid another visit to Dominica. Two girls arrived from Canada for two weeks to help in children's work on the island. This came about from reports in Missionary magazines that were circulated among the assemblies of Canada. They had heard of Petite Savanne and had arranged to go there for two weeks to help with children's work. I took them there in the car and felt for them having to stay in a very primitive village. After three days, I wondered how they were getting on and decided to pay them a visit. After the gruelling three hour journey I arrived at the hall and one of the girls ran to me with joy, yet in great distress. The mosquitoes and other things had made her quite ill and she was praying that someone would come and take her back to Roseau - and then I came. The other girl was determined to stay in spite of the difficulties. She managed to remain for the full two weeks. Both of them helped greatly in the children's work and left the believers much better organised. The first girl did a good job in Roseau and other places during their visit. They left when the two weeks were up and felt they had done a good work. So they had. I met one of the girls many years later when I was visiting the assemblies in Canada. She informed me that she could never forget the visit to Dominica and how it helped her in her Christian experience.

I had the privilege of working with brother Peter Simms for a while. He took me to help in his prison work. I have mentioned already how dreadful the conditions were for the prisoners. I was able to see for myself the cramped cells and the strict discipline. Most of the prisoners were very tough characters and the wardens even tougher. Quite a few of the prisoners were in for long sentences for murder. The Lord worked in the gospel and a number had trusted in the Lord Jesus as their Saviour. We preached the gospel to about fifty men and then had a session of Bible teaching to those who professed to be saved. We had a visit like this about every ten days. Perhaps some could question their salvation but many of them when set at liberty sought out Christian fellowship. One or two of the Christian dominations had settled on the island, but Mr. Sam McCune was the pioneer who opened the trail. One man had completed his sentence and was released after my visit. He immediately got baptised and came into the fellowship with the believers. I will always remember this excellent work. Peter was dedicated to this and would let nothing stand in his way. I often thought no one else had the personality to do this service like Peter Simms.

Peter and I had a series with the gospel in the hall in Roseau. I did not have far to journey to the meetings, just up a flight of stairs from the basement! We went round visiting most days - quite an experience in a good sense. All doors were open because of the heat. Some people were sitting in their little lots outside and all were ready to talk. Never once were we turned away. Rather all were pleased to see us. Little children were running about all round us. I was told that the greater part of the population were children under the age of twelve. Morals were very slack on Dominica and other islands at that time, but perhaps are improved somewhat at this present time. Few living together were married and when a man got tired with the woman in his house, he just sent her off and replaced her with another woman. Hence, children were in abundance.

I noticed something that was not only the case in Dominica but in all the islands I visited. In terrible heat and although most houses were without bathrooms, the folk and the children were very clean. There was never the slightest hint of body odour, and their clothing was spotless. The women daily washed the family clothes in the river and left them on the rocks to dry. Drying took a very short time indeed. Also the little girls had wonderful hairdos which must have taken hours to do each day. Wonderful and very happy people, is all I could say.

As for the gospel meetings, I never had an experience like this in my life. The crowds came every night, mothers with their children, grandfathers and grandmothers. The numbers increased night by night and we ran out of seats to accommodate them. We made an appeal that people had to come early to find a seat and if one came later they would have to bring their own seating. This resulted in people turning up with all kinds of chairs, stools, dining chairs and large armchairs perched upon their heads. The armchairs took up a lot of room and some people stood outside the entire meeting each evening. I was amazed at the preaching of Peter Simms. He spoke of people counting their rosary beads and falling down into hell and suchlike. This he did with a very loud voice. He continually spoke against the deception of the Roman Catholic Church. I thought this would turn the people off for all were Roman Catholic. However, this did not deter them, and still they came. The Lord added His blessing to the meetings and put the hall in Roseau on the map as one would say. There is one little incident I have thought of many times that took place during these gospel meetings. A pretty little girl about sixteen years of age attended the meetings every night and always sat in the same seat. She came early to get this seat. Her name was Rosie. I met her in a street in Roseau one afternoon and I passed the remark that she had been to the meetings. She informed me that she had never missed a night so far. I asked her whether she understood the message of the gospel. She answered that she knew the message very well indeed. I said, "Have you got saved yet?" and she answered "No". I said, "Do you not understand that Christ alone can save?" Her answer was so sad, "I have not asked Him to be my Saviour yet". I asked her why and she just dropped her head. However, she still came to the meetings and I was glad to see that. Then I discovered what did hinder her as to salvation. There was a dance held each evening in a certain building and the young people danced to the loud beating of the music into the early morning. Rosie was found there dancing the night through. She went there shortly after she had been to the gospel meeting.

After the meetings, I had some Bible Readings and ministry over the other three of the assemblies.

I made many very dear friends. I must mention a few. First there was Ferrier Bruno. He was the best-taught man on the island. He had lived a dreadful life before he was saved. Like all the young men he was very much of the flesh and lived a very immoral life. He was able to read and made a study of the Scriptures from the moment of his conversion. He could have graced any conference platform. Yet he was without any Christian books. He had heard of a Scofield Bible and longed to possess one. I often listened to him and came to the conclusion he was God taught. We got on wonderfully together. He usually called on me most mornings in the prophet's chamber for a talk on the Word. He delighted in this. The five assemblies each had a conference during the year and he was the principal speaker. Like the others, he was poor with a large family.

Another brother that impressed me was Merrill Matthews. He was a school teacher and was a great help in the assembly to which he belonged and to the others as well. He too was a capable speaker at meetings. One day when we were enjoying a walk together he told me his conversion. I was very impressed with it. He had been walking through a little village and had seen a pretty girl walking along. Now he like others was fond of the girls! He had joined her and had noticed a book under her arm. To engage a conversation, he had asked her what the book was that she had under her arm. Her answer had been, "It is the Word of God". She had then informed him that the book told her about the love of God and the forgiveness of sins. On hearing this, he told me, his interest was then in that book and not the girl. After a while the girl had arrived at his house. He had asked her for a loan of the book. "It is the Bible", she had said, adding, "I will lend it to you for two weeks only. At the end of two weeks please bring the Bible back to me". Merrill had taken the Bible and he with a friend had read the Scriptures each evening for the two weeks. Through the Holy Spirit they both had learned the truth of Salvation in Christ alone and both were saved. On returning the book as he had promised, he had asked the girl where he could obtain a Bible. The girl had given him the address of Peter Simms. The two young men had sought out Peter and had asked for Bibles. He had given them one each. He had also asked them, "Do you know how to read this book?" Both had admitted they needed help. Peter had then met up with them a night each week and had taught them. They had been good students and had quickly responded and had learnt many truths including that of meeting together with others like minded. In a little time after these things Merrill had sought the fellowship of the assembly. I do not have the information on the outcome of his friend. There were other dear brethren and sisters that were examples of their faith. To tell their stories would indeed take another book.

Now I must make a few remarks about the people of Dominica. There was no real industry on the island. Almost all lived by the labour of the field. A few were engaged in fishing. The food was simple but healthy, an abundance of fruit and vegetables, fish, mountain chicken and plain bread that was sort of tasteless. Cakes, sweets and the things we all enjoy at home were seldom to be found. There were no McDonald's or Kentucky Fried Chicken at that time. There was only one hotel; there had been another one on the water's edge which was destroyed by Hurricane David. No doubt things have developed very much since then.

I found a place that sometimes sold ice-cream in Roseau. Happy day! All this made the people to be very healthy and happy. Few people possessed a car. There was a heavy tax on cars on the island but not for vans that could be used for commerce. The people were without any public transport and as most of the villages were built on slopes, the people had to walk wherever they wanted to go. This resulted in a good thing: most of the children and the older people were very healthy, especially with very well-developed legs. I remember in one particular meeting an old man was always present who wore short trousers. His body was thin and wasted but his leg muscles were developed from thigh to ankle. As noted before, the people were born with intelligence, good memories and they were thus easy to teach. Maybe the nourishing food had something to do with this.

I noticed on the next visits I made to Dominica many men possessed vans which they used to carry tourists around the island. This was due to the cruise ships visiting the island. Tourism helped the economy of the country. However, they were poor drivers. They seldom if ever dipped headlights. Often they would pass when there was little room to do so. Driving at night in Dominica became a nightmare. On my first visit I found that phones were only in the Post Office. I phoned my wife in Northern Ireland a few times. It cost me about ten pounds as well as a very long wait to use it. I wrote letters instead. It is about forty years since I first was in Dominica and all will have changed since then.

With the abundant rainfall, the rivers at times changed their course. The increased flow of waters down the hills overflowed at times and took the easier way down. The map of Dominica needed changes to be made from time to time. This brought surveyors to the island. During my first visit, a brother from Newcastle in Northern Ireland called Adair came for a few weeks to do surveying work. He had a four wheel drive Land Rover. He came to the meetings in Roseau and remembered the Lord with us. One day we planned a picnic as Sally McCune had received a nice cake in a parcel from some sisters at home. I iced the cake as I was a baker to trade. The three of us went on a trip up a steep mountain road which soon ran out. We just travelled over grass and little bushes until we came to a large lake. This had formed in an extinct volcano crater.

On our way we came across a white man with a haversack on his back walking up the steep path. It was a rare thing to see a white man far up the hills and alone in Dominica and we offered him a lift. He refused in quite a rough manner. "Let me alone!", he cried, so we continued on our journey. After we had stopped for a while to admire the landscape, the man overtook us, stopped and apologised. He then informed us that he came from Norway for a month every year to get away from a very busy life. He was a director of a very large business, one of these executives who work day and night, a phone always in their hand. He came to Dominica to get a time of peace away from phones and office. He just wanted to be left alone and to enjoy nature in the wild all around him. I asked him where he dwelt. He informed us that he had a tent further up the hill and a little black boy came to him every second day and brought him his food etc. that he had ordered the previous time he was with him. The lad made the journey on foot, about five miles uphill all the way, and the man paid the lad well indeed. Then he continued on his journey to his tent wherever it was pitched.

At last we got to the place where we intended to picnic. As I have noted, this was a very large lake with the water as smooth as glass. All about the place and around the lake very large flowers were growing. They looked like tulips, but very much larger. They stood about a foot or more from the ground and the large cup of each flower was filled with water. We found this very handy washing up after our picnic. We just bent the stem and a large quantity of fresh water poured out. I remarked that not even a bird was to be seen. The total silence was most soothing. We enjoyed our lunch and a little walk afterward partly round the lake and then started for home. This little experience is something I often think of. I understand the man from Norway coming all that way to enjoy the solitude. We missed brother Adair when the time came for him to depart from Dominica as his work was completed there.

In all I visited Dominica seven times and for the last few my wife Betsy accompanied me. She just loved Dominica and the other islands. The mosquitoes loved her but she did not by any means love them. One bite was very severe. It was on her eyelid and she suffered a few days with this before it began to heal. Betsy was most useful in children's work and was kept very busy with this. Sally McCune saw to that.

I remember one time in Petite Savanne a brother was being baptised and for this they used a concrete bath big enough to baptise even a large person. This was built outside the hall. It had to be cleaned out before being used for a baptism, as people that lived about used it as a litter bin. There was a large mansion of a house on a hill on the outskirts of the village and the owner just happened to pass by when the brethren were cleaning out the concrete pit. He stopped his car and inquired what they were doing. They explained about the baptism. The gentleman told them to make use of his swimming pool beside the house. It was a very hot day and about forty of the believers made the climb to the swimming pool in the garden of the large house. The pool was a very large one and all the believers gathered round the pool. A few young people were baptised just in their clothes and then came out of the water and stood in the sunshine to dry. Every one continued to stand around the pool and I whispered to my wife, "I know what is going to happen now". A pool like this was something they had never seen in their lives. So they stood, then a brother dived into the pool followed by about three more then all dived into the water and had great fun swimming about for about half an hour. After their swim they just stood in the sun and were dried in about five minutes. I will always remember this happy experience. From that time on the believers all looked forward to a baptism!

I remember another time when my wife was with me that I was booked for a Lord's Day in one of the assemblies in Salisbury. Sally McCune took us in her car. It was about twenty miles from Roseau. After the breaking of the bread meeting, I ministered the Word. We all had a lovely time of fellowship. The three of us were invited to a good brother's house, the home of Frederick with his wife and their pretty little children. He was the builder who helped build the hall and other halls. In later years they built an apartment beside their house for Mrs. McCune. They always called her Mrs. McCune. Sally often used this as the apartment in

Roseau was used by other visitors. After a very enjoyable dinner, Sally announced that she was going back to Roseau. Then said I, "What about me? I have a ministry and a gospel meeting here later in the day". When Sally McCune wanted to do something, nothing would stop her and that was so in this case. For some reason, she wanted to leave me behind. Frederick and his wife said that it was all right. They had a spare bedroom and they would love to keep me. He would take me back to Roseau in the morning. So my wife and Sally departed and left me with the good friends.

I took the two meetings and the numbers that attended were very good. The work was still going on from its beginning, the first assembly in Dominica.

After supper and a talk together all went to bed. My bedroom was very sparse indeed. It contained a bed and a chair and, if I remember right, a little table of some sort. So I hung my clothes on some hooks on the door, got into bed, read the Scriptures and turned off the light as the switch was just above my head. Now the bed was more like a hammock. It dipped in the middle and after about fifteen minutes I switched on the light to see if I could make myself more comfortable. To my great distress, an army of cockroaches were climbing up the walls all round the room and some were scattered over the floor. Once I turned on the light, they all scattered down slits between the floor and the walls. I was horrified. To me the only resource was to burn the light the night through which I did. I slept some and I sat up at times and studied the Scriptures and so I managed to get the night through. Another thing, in most of the West Indies the walls of the houses stop about a foot from the ceiling. The reason for this is to let fresh air circulate around the rooms. I could hear everything in the house throughout the night, including the children using the toilet and the sound of snoring.

In the morning, I told Frederick about the cockroaches. "They are harmless beings", he answered. "We are used to them." Well, they had lived with them all their lives on the island. This was not the case with me, so we let it rest. After a very good breakfast, we started out in his open-backed van for Roseau, as he had to do some business there. Now, at that time, there was no public transport on the island. Things may have changed since then. It was the custom for people to stand at the corner and thumb a lift to wherever they were going. Every driver fell in with this idea and stopped to give a lift to the children going to school or other folk going into the town. Frederick stopped and about six boys and girls leapt into the back of his truck. We stopped again and lifted some more young people going to school. The back of the truck was overcrowded but nobody minded. We came to a very steep hill and the truck with its load stopped. Many of the boys and girls leapt off and pushed the truck up the hill and off we started again.

A funny thing happened after this which I will always remember. In due time we came near Roseau and Frederick stopped for a man and a woman who had a large plaster which was the length of her leg. There was no room on the back of the truck so they got into the front cab. So there were four of us in the cab of the truck and the woman could not bend her leg as the plaster extended to above her knee. So she just stuck her leg out of the window and we travelled to Roseau in the crushed condition. I could hardly breathe. I was very glad to see the hall in Roseau and was welcomed with another breakfast in the apartment. I complained to Sally about leaving me to the primitive conditions - cockroaches and all. Her retort was that the experience would harden me for work in the West Indies. I was not too sure of her methods! Looking back it was a wonderful experience and I smile to myself when I think of this occasion.

As I have already mentioned, conferences were happy occasions in Dominica. They were very well attended with a cross section from all the five assemblies plus others who had lately got saved. I was at one particular conference and a speaker had been invited from another island. I looked round the company and Sally with myself were the only white people. The company numbered about three hundred. There was Sally McCune, a little old lady sitting amongst them, and I thought: all this started with her. The Lord had honoured her with this large company of saved ones who all loved her very dearly. Truly the Lord had worked and the gospel of God was indeed the power of God unto salvation. These beloved believers had been saved from darkness and immorality and were now living for the Lord Jesus as their Lord.

After one of the local brethren spoke, the visiting brother then spoke. After reading the Scriptures and saying a few words, he said with a very loud voice that they did not need white people on the islands."We are capable of doing without them. We can teach ourselves" - and so he ranted and raved. There was not an "Amen" to be heard anywhere in the company. After he ranted and raved a while, he got down from the platform. Then I got up to speak and every brother and sister in the building shouted a loud "AMEN!" I then knew that the opinion of the former speaker was not by any means the conviction of the dear beloved saints of Dominica. In all my travels with the assemblies of the West Indies I never came across any prejudice against the white believers, except for this occasion. We all just saw and loved each one as being in Christ, a heaven-born people.

I often think of another occasion when Sally McCune left me and went home, taking my wife with her. This happened in Petite Savanne. We made the journey that I might have another opportunity to minister the Scriptures with them. All the beloved saints were present and I spoke for about an hour. No one told me what was happening next, but the brethren began to arrange the seats. Sally McCune said good-night to me and with my wife started for Roseau. The brethren had arranged a Bible Reading after the ministry and all seemed to know this except myself. The Bible Reading started about nine o'clock in the evening and continued for a long time. I was getting tired as the time now had reached 11 o'clock. I said that I thought the Reading had gone on long enough. They mumbled among themselves and decided to continue for another half hour. I then tried to finish the meeting, remarking that the dear sisters were bound to be very tired. However, the meeting continued until midnight then all went home. I stayed with the brother with his family of girls for the night. One of the brethren who had a van took me back to Roseau the next morning.

During my second visit to Dominica, I realized that the brethren had very few books of an expository nature to help them with their studies. No Bible Book shop existed on the island and if a book was wanted they had to send to the United States. All this cost money plus the postage and it was out of the question as they had little money to spare.

I knew a dear brother in the States who sold Christian books at a giveaway price. He got these from Christian publishers and the books had a little flaw that very few would notice. Perhaps a mistake in the numbering of the pages and such-like. I sent this brother a hundred pounds to buy as many good books as he could and to send them to me in Dominica. This was announced in the American assembly the brother belonged to and they added another two hundred dollars to this. Eventually two large boxes arrived containing almost two hundred of the best of books. How to distribute the books was another problem. The brethren suggested that every brother who was interested and could read could take a few each, then exchange with each other after a month or so. This plan was carried out and the books were very well used. They proved to be a blessing to many.

I remember another time Sally McCune received a gift of fifty pounds from some sisters in Northern Ireland. She changed this into Dominican dollars. Then we went to the local supermarket, which was only a hut in comparison to the supermarkets in Northern Ireland, and spent all the money on groceries. I thought that we were going to fare well over the next week or so. However, we went to the home of a dear brother who was out of work. He had a large family. We entered the house and the dear wife told us she could not provide any refreshment as the cupboards were empty. We then brought in all the groceries and there was great joy in that house. It was the pattern of Sally to consider others first with any money she received. She saved some now and again but always for a purpose. When she finally came home to Belfast she had no pension or any other means of living except the gifts from the Lord's people. Being at home instead of on the islands, she did not receive very much in those days. My wife Betsy took this matter up and after much form filling and interviews Mrs. Sally McCune received a pension from the government. This proved to be a great help to her in her closing days.

When I left my wife and family for the first missionary journey, I took only one hundred pounds with me. I left enough for my wife and family to live on until I returned. However, the assemblies in Dominica were very poor and I never received any gifts from any assembly in Dominica during the time I was there. Now I felt that I had to put money in the box on the Lord's Day and soon my money was down to almost the last pound - and I will write what happened after that. First, however, I must sum up the work and condition of the Christians in Dominica.

The island was primitive yet beautiful. The view from the sea was a picture of high mountains covered with greenery and the little towns and villages built from shore to high up the hills. Most of the people were poor but happy. They dressed daily in clean clothes and were very clean living in many ways. Food that was imported was very expensive and seldom found in the homes of most of the people. The coming of the gospel made a great difference to those who believed. Life and love shone out of the faces of many.

Some brethren had to learn to read and write before they could study the Scriptures for themselves. They learned the principles of the assembly and practised them in a most Scriptural way.

Brother Merrill Matthews for his work in school was sent to England for some dedicational work and felt that the assemblies there were not as Scriptural as those in his homeland. Peter Simms was a great help to them as was also Ken Taylor although I did not get to know this dear brother as well as Peter Simms.

The assemblies were very well developed with an excellent exercise in all of the meetings. Most of the brethren could take part most acceptably and this helped everyone present. All were most strict about fellowship. There was no attempt to increase the numbers by taking in anyone who applied. I noticed on my first visit that the numbers sitting at the back of the hall at the breaking of the bread were greater that those who remembered the Lord. I asked the question, "Who are these?" I was informed that the people sitting at the back were folk who had got saved, but their lives were so mixed up that they could not be accepted in fellowship. Most of these were to do with the marriage state, or rather lack of it. Most folk living with each other had families and were never married. This had to be set right before fellowship was accepted. With the men folk this was easily solved. Generally speaking, the woman was willing to get married to their partner as this made for security. With the woman, it was difficult. Her partner would be still an unbeliever and not willing to get married. She could either stay or leave with her children and the man would soon have another woman in the house to take her place. Thus the dear sister was without support. Few of the women then made the decision to leave.

I remember one dear sister who had three children. She was living with a man as a partner. Her name was Agatha and when she got saved she asked the man living with her to marry her. He refused, so she felt before the Lord that this state could not continue. She left him and he sent her three children away also with her. In this destitute state, Sally McCune took her in for a week or so, and then met the rent payment for a little house for them. This arrangement was only temporary. Sally could not continue to pay this rent. A new Bank was just built in Roseau and soon to open. Agatha applied for the cleaning job that was advertised and was successful in obtaining the position. The manager came to her and told her that a house was part of the job. So she ended up with a free house and a salary. The Lord honoured her indeed. Such a testimony of the grace of God.

In all I paid about seven visits to Dominica and loved every one of them. The scenic island was pleasant to the eyes, I liked the food, and I never had sickness of any kind all the times I was there. However, above all I just loved the people and was very contented and blessed with my fellowship with the saints. Now I must go back to that first visit and the second island I was on. This was a totally different experience.

6 Barbados

On my first visit to Dominica and after the gospel meetings in Roseau and other meetings, I had a meeting every night except Saturday. These were both gospel and trying to teach the beloved saints. I was feeling somewhat tired. One Friday night at supper, Sally McCune said to me, "We are going to Barbados in the morning as you need a little rest". This was just typical of Sally. The thing was just sprung upon you whether you liked it or not. I told her that I was down to my last pound and could not pay for this and she then produced the tickets. Early Saturday morning, we were found at the little airport waiting for the LIAT flight to Barbados. It turned out to be a larger plane than what was generally used between the islands. I knew then that Barbados must be a popular island. All the arrangements as to where we would stay and so forth had been made by Sally unbeknown to me. I was looking forward to a little rest and perhaps a swim or two as beaches were scarce in Dominica. The flight lasted about an hour and on landing I saw that the runway was very long indeed. Everything I could see was on a larger scale compared to Dominica. The airport occupied a very large area and was open on two sides at least. The fresh air could be felt; the large roof kept out the sunlight and with rows of pillars to the street instead of walls. This made the place very comfortable. Huge jets were coming in all the time and hundreds of people were spilling out of the arrival lounge. We were met by the dear lady in whose house we were to stay. She was a remarkable woman called Nell Archer, a dear friend of Sally

McCune. A taxi was waiting for us, paid for by Nell. The contrast between Barbados and Dominica was remarkable. At the time I was in Dominica the population numbered a little over 72,000. It is just about the same today. The population of Barbados when I visited at the first was almost 300,000 and again it is just about the same today. On the other hand, the area of Dominica is 751 square kilometres, over against that of Barbados which is only 439 square kilometres. This means that Barbados had more than four times the number of people living on about half the area of Dominica.

The airport was in Bridgetown, which indeed was more like a city than a town. We made the journey to Nell's house and the sea was by our side all the way. The sidewalks were full of smiling people, both black and white, and restaurants and shops of every kind could be seen as we passed by in the taxi. The taxi driver was a very friendly chap, just like most of the people we came across during our short stay.

A few remarks about Barbados might be helpful at this point.

Barbados is likely the most prosperous island of the West Indies. Houses were grand; roads were so much superior to Dominica; there was even a ring road that ran for quite a few miles around Bridgetown. Cars were everywhere, mostly of American or Japanese make. Cars from Britain and Europe were very scarce indeed. I only saw about three during my stay in Barbados. Most of the brethren and sisters in the assemblies had their own car. Quite a number of people had two houses, one would be rented out and the other they lived in. Many rich people and world celebrities possessed houses on a particular section just out of Bridgetown. These houses were in the million pound range - from about five to twenty million pounds. I saw some of these and they were magnificent. The house Nell lived was a very grand building, more about this later. One of the things that helped Barbados was the tourist trade. Cruise ships anchored in the harbour daily. Some days up to three large ships visited the island. This brought thousands of people pouring into Bridgetown and around the country. Beside this, quite a number of large jet planes landed at the airport carrying hundreds of people from Europe, America and elsewhere. Tourism in Dominica was nothing like this; only about three thousand yearly sought to visit the island. Now this was when I was there more than forty years ago. Barbados had everything that Dominica did not have to encourage tourism. There was only one beach in Dominica and the sand was kind of blackish, but in Barbados the beaches were ringed right round the island and the sand was excellent with little or no stones and nice and soft. The beaches in some places stretched for miles. They were lined with hotels and apartments which are rented out to people who stay for several months at a time. People from Europe and North America owned houses on the island and stayed there during the winter months to get away from the cold weather in their home countries.

The weather was beautiful and sunny all the year round. There was a continual sea breeze that kept the island cool. Local people called this "Nature's Air Conditioning". As to eating out, the choice was enormous. Some of the American chain restaurants, such as McDonald's, were there. Many hotels and stores provided food. Again, there were some very interesting restaurants that one does not often see; one on the shore was made out of half of a large sailing ship cut right down the middle. Naturally it was called "The Ship Restaurant". I just loved to dine in that place. There was a very large department store in Bridgetown called "Cave Shepherd" that sold everything one could wish to buy. This store was furnished with a very large and lovely restaurant on the top floor. The food was excellent and the price most reasonable. We ate there very often on our first visit and many times on future visits. This was the place to go when downtown, as they say. The police force was excellent and very helpful. People were safe when out in the evenings. The darkness fell suddenly about 6 to 6.30pm and people wandered about to midnight in many places. Over the many visits I made to Barbados, I met many believers there on holiday from Canada, America and elsewhere.

As for Nell, she was a most interesting lady and a wonderful Christian. There was only one Nell in my opinion - and others would have agreed with me. Nell was born into a very wealthy family who owned the wholesale chemist business in Barbados. She never had to work in her life. She never had to be under any employer or such like. Housework was all done by others; she was brought up with servants and maids in her home. Eventually, her parents died and she inherited a large sum of money plus a lovely five bedroomed colonial house in very posh district on the edge of Bridgetown.

She was a believer and had a great interest in the Scriptures. On inheriting the money, she took herself off to the Dallas Theological Seminary. She studied Greek etc. there for three years. This used up a good part of her money. After this, she did some travelling across Asia and Australia and other places of interest. Eventually, she got a letter from her solicitors saying that her money was all spent and to come home. She must have thought that her money would last forever! On arriving home, she had this large house and little money to run it. She decided to take in paying guests to help her financial situation. Hence she kept her long loved friend Sally and myself. On subsequent trips to Barbados, I always stayed with Nell and the assemblies paid for my keep.

Nell was very slow in anything to do with housework. To her everything to do with housework was a high mountain to be climbed. It took her almost an hour to boil an egg. The reason for this was she was so afraid of germs, so every utensil that was used had to be scrubbed several times. I remember one Sunday at dinner time we finally got the dinner at five in the afternoon. We had purchased a chicken which we had for dinner, but Nell washed that chicken so many times it was nearly worn away. She went over the skin so thoroughly looking for hairs and so on. Preparing the potatoes and vegetables also took such a long time, washed and rewashed so many times that finally after about five hours in the kitchen dinner was ready. Alas, the dinner was cold;

it took her such a long time to dish it out! She had a little woman for a servant to help her cook etc. Her name was Barrel; she was a very sweet little black lady. She often winked at me and lifted up her eyes behind Nell's back at the time Nell took to do the simplest task. I will never understand why Nell did not let Barrel make the dinner. No doubt we would have had our meal on time. With all this, you could not help loving Nell. She was clever in some things and very slow at other things, especially in housework. I think she kept the maid because the family always had servants in the house. I laughed to myself on many occasions. When sitting at the table, Nell would drop her fork onto the floor. She shouted for Barrel to come and lift her fork for her and Barrel would come down the very long hall from the kitchen muttering to herself. Nell would then say, "Stop muttering and lift me this fork". Barrel, very much out of breath, would stoop, lift the fork and hand it to Nell. Then Nell would explode, "Go wash the fork first". Things like this happened at every meal. Sally McCune just sat there and patiently waited. Afterword she would say to me, "Now that is just Nell!"

Over against all this, Nell had an appetite for the Scriptures that few could equal. After meals and long into the evening after the meeting, I was bombarded with questions from her. I had to explain something several ways before she was able to grasp the meaning of a passage. It was hard work, but I enjoyed her enthusiasm. Would there were many like her! With all this, she was one of the kindest people I ever met. Again, I say, there was only one Nell.

We arrived in early afternoon and were supposed to stay there in Barbados for one week, but it turned out that we stayed for a second week. After talking to Nell and being introduced to an old lady, one of Nell's paying guests, I unpacked and had a refreshing wash. Later Sally and I went down the road that Nell lived on which shortly joined a main road that led into the town and to a lovely beach. The sea was on one side and homes and shops on the other. We came to a Kentucky Fried Chicken branch. How wonderful to see this, no such thing in Dominica! We went in and had something to eat and bought some for Nell and the lady staying with her and started back to Nell's house. Just outside the door of the KFC we met a very handsome brother who recognised Sally immediately. Sally McCune introduced me to him and explained that I had come from Northern Ireland on a visit to Dominica. He then invited me to a meeting later that night in a hall about four miles away to give a word of ministry. He called for us and took the three of us - Sally, Nell and me - to the meeting in his car.

The hall was by the seaside in a quaint little village where the folk fished and sold what they had caught on the shore to a lot of shoppers passing by. There were about sixty people at the meeting that night, some from this host assembly and a few from other halls. After about twenty minutes of prayer, I gave a word from one of the Gospels. They thought the teaching was very profitable. There were some refreshments after the meeting and I was encircled by believers asking me questions on the Scriptures. One of the brethren who came from the largest assembly on the Island asked me what I was doing for the rest of the week. I told him I was free all week. He answered, "You are not free now; you are coming to our hall for the rest of the week". He was a leading elder in the Dayrells Road assembly, the one that Nell attended. So, my little rest did not materialize. I was quite happy about the arrangement. After all, I came to help with the Word on the islands.

We went to Dayrells Road to remember the Lord on Lord's Day morning. The hall was full. It seemed that every seat was taken, a large number indeed, far beyond any of the assemblies in Dominica. I gave a word after the breaking of the bread. In the evening I preached the gospel to a full hall. It was announced that I would be there for ministry for the rest of that week. I decided to take up 1 Corinthians. I thought this line would be suitable,

Gospel Hall, Barbados

especially the wonderful truths for the assemblies that are found therein.

The first night there were about a hundred people present. The next night, the company numbered about two hundred. The last three nights, the place was overcrowded. Extra seating was arranged and every seat occupied. The last two nights the people were lined around the walls of the hall and many stood outside and listened as every window was opened and the door as well. It was like a revival and lots of young brethren and sisters were present. The brethren told me they had not seen the like of this for over forty years. Before the Friday night meeting started, the brethren asked me to stay and to continue with 1 Corinthians. However, the meetings would be held in the largest hall that was situated in Bridgetown. This hall also had a large gallery and could seat five hundred or more people. The Lord seemed to be working: the interest was extraordinary and the numbers increased each night. After each meeting, young believers gather round me with intelligent questions almost for an hour. The last two nights, the hall was full to capacity, every seat on the gallery as well as in the hall and many had to stand. I really enjoyed the singing; it was marvellous, with great volume and harmony. I learned later that the believers could sing every hymn of the *Redemption Songs* hymn book. On the last night of the meetings, which was on the Friday night, the large company sang the hymn, "God be with you till we meet again". It was a most moving experience, many of the dear believers were weeping. We were flying back to Dominica in the morning but the saints did not want me to depart from them and I felt the same about them. Sally put this in a quaint way saying, "A few people would have been needed to go round after the meeting to mop up the tears that was shed in the singing of that last hymn". The next morning we headed for the airport and found about twenty believers there to see us off. This increased to about thirty by the time we were to depart. They stood in a large circle in the midst of a very busy airport and had a prayer meeting. People carrying large items of luggage had to walk round the circle of praying people. Again, some tears were shed. The brethren made me promise to return and I said I would do so.

Now, a few points about this first visit to Barbados. The first night of our stay in the house of Nell, the little lady that paid her way to stay with Nell offered me a book to read as I went to bed. The book was entitled, "The Life of Hudson Taylor". "You will find this a very useful book", she told me. I took the book to please her. I had other material with me that I intended to read. When I opened the door of my bedroom, I spied a large lizard resting on my pillow. These are harmless but I did not like them, especially one in my bed. I tried to frighten it away by waving my arms about and talking, but it just sat looking at me. I then took the book in my hand about Hudson Taylor and gently pushed the lizard off my bed. The lizard did not fall off the bed but disappeared behind the pillow onto the frame of the bed. I got on my knees and there I saw the lizard sitting on the frame of my bed. Now the people of the island would have caught it by the tail and thrown it out, but I could not do this having no knowledge of lizards and suchlike. So again I gave it a gentle tap with the book. It fell to the ground and was still. I moved it with the book and found the creature had died, yet I really pushed it rather than hit it. I then opened the book and used the cover as a shovel to lift up the lizard and throw it out of the open window. I slept soundly then after the day of travel and the meeting in Cherry Grove. Next morning at breakfast the little lady asked me if I had found the book on Hudson Taylor a useful book. I answered that it had turned out to be very useful indeed. I then returned the book to her.

During the two weeks, I made many good friends. They took Sally and me out for delicious meals in many well-known places to eat in Barbados. One brother and sister brought me to the boat restaurant which I mentioned earlier in this book. The food was "out of this world", as the saying goes. I was also taken to other restaurants that were very posh and expensive. All were very kind to us; the people would take you out and pay for a meal rather than bring you to their houses for some reason. On one occasion the folk asked us out and to our joy others from the assembly in Dayrells Road were also invited. We then had the pleasure of dining with 10-14 believers. We talked and enjoyed the Scriptures after we had eaten. So, we had the double portion!

Another point, I have written of the fact that my money was down to the last few Caribbean dollars. After the first night of ministry at Cherry Grove, the brethren passed on to me a gift of 50 American dollars. On Sunday morning at Dayrells Road there was a couple from Belfast. They were on a cruise ship that had stayed in Barbados for the day. This pair were believers who came to the breaking of bread and Nell invited them to her house for dinner after the meeting. We had a lovely time together with folk from home although I did not know them personally. We had a talk together after dinner and the man asked me if I was on holiday. I told him I was there for a while to try and help the believers with Bible teaching. On leaving for their ship, the brother took me aside and told me I was doing a good work. He pushed something into the pocket of my coat. This turned out to be a hundred pound note! How good and faithful the God whom we serve. I had told no one of the fact that my money was diminished and now I had 100 pounds and fifty American dollars. The Lord is good and before the end of the two weeks in Barbados, between gifts from the two assemblies and personal gifts from the saints, I left Barbados with almost 1000 US dollars and the 100 pounds from the brother from Belfast. I had still a number of weeks in Dominica before I set out for home. I offered Sally McCune help with the return fares to Barbados but she refused as I knew she would!

My experience of Barbados was in contrast to my later visits to other islands in the Caribbean. The better roads, the shops and restaurants and, above all, the people. They were friendly, happy and the gospel had worked among so many people. The Pentecostal folk were numerous in Barbados. On the Lord's Day, you could hear the singing of about two thousand people who had gathered in a large church building not far from the city centre. Baptist people also were there in good numbers. The Seventh Day Adventists had made a strong impression on many and they were getting stronger year by year. One of the reasons for this was that they imported gifted men from the United States. These men had the ability of holding an audience spellbound with words. When on another visit at Easter time and again in the house of Nell, I heard one of these men on the television. The man spoke on the sufferings of Christ with tremendous emotion. Even Nell was moved to tears when listening to this man on the television. The speaker stayed in Barbados for a week or so and the crowds that attended his meetings were tremendous. The brethren of the assemblies of Barbados knew that they needed strong Bible teaching above anything else to build the assemblies in the truth. I remember a dear brother who told me several times after the meetings that what the believers needed was not quaint stories to amuse but Bible teaching to profit.

I came to Barbados without any knowledge of the assembly situation in that beautiful island. I soon learnt all that I needed to know. At that time there were twelve assemblies in Barbados, some small with a dozen or less in fellowship and others with between thirty to a few hundred in fellowship. They all were in harmony. This presented a united testimony to all the people round about. Some differed in many ways but they still kept the unity. No assembly would cut off another because of something they differed upon. One helpful thing I noticed was that they all supported each other. If one assembly had a series of meetings the other assembles mostly closed their meeting to support that series. I saw this in action time and again. On a later visit, I had three nights with a little assembly in a small village with about ten in fellowship. I remember the first night. There were about twenty present when the leading brother gave out the opening hymn. Before we had finished singing, a large bus appeared at the front door and about fifty folk came into the meeting. When all were seated, he opened with prayer. He was not on the platform but in the second seat from the front. Two more buses arrived and the people were coming in and looking for seats. The brother prayed on. Two brethren, one on each side of the platform, were waving their arms about pointing out seats. The beloved brother prayed on. The hall was now packed and some looking for seats bumped into the dear brother who was standing praying. He just prayed on. I saw all this and was on the point of laughing out. I had to control myself. Still they came in and stood anywhere they could find a spot. Brethren and sisters were standing, waving their arms about to point out seats. Others stood on the seats to be seen and whispered, as they thought, saying, "There is a seat here". The beloved brother continued to pray. When he at last finished, he was almost pushed into a corner and was flabbergasted with the full hall. By now they were standing outside. So, he made everyone welcome and I started to minister with a smile. The same "pantomime" took place the next two nights. It was so amusing I could never forget the nightly scramble for seats amid the brother standing to pray. The Lord helped with the Word and we had a wonderful time of blessing. I thanked the Lord for this wonderful interest in the Word of God. Would we had the same interest in the homeland! This would indeed build up the believers and make them to be channels of blessing to others. They would be lights that shone in the darkness. About one third of the folk that attended were young brethren and sisters in Christ. I understand that after the meeting many of these young ones would crowd into a McDonald's or KFC to enjoy fellowship together. Sometimes they sang hymns in testimony to others. Now all this is an example of how the assemblies worked together. Dayrells Road assembly hired a bus to take the saints to the meetings the three nights as did other assemblies.

Gospel Tent, Barbados

I saw this unity at work on a later visit. I was having a gospel series in a large tent in connection with Dayrells Road. Each night one of the assemblies had the responsibility of chairing the meeting. The elders from that assembly would sit on the platform. One would see to the singing and another would open in prayer and so on. Now there was an assembly that had slipped back somewhat that would have had a part in the gospel series and it may have been better had they not been involved, but when I questioned the elders of Dayrells Road as to why they still had fellowship with them, the answer they gave me was, "If we did that, we would never get them restored to the right principles. Things would just get worse. Departure would continue". A few months later, that particular assembly saw their folly and got back to the right principles. All were in harmony again. I thought this was wisdom indeed. A lot of prayer and teaching, individual to individual, brought about the recovery.

Bathsheba

Airy Hill

Cherry Grove
(Ch8)

Dayrells Road,
Crumpton St and
Fairfield Gospel
Hall (Ch8)

Bridgetown

Stream
Gospel Hall

Further Visits to Barbados

n all I made about nine further trips to Barbados. On some occasions I took in a visit to another island that had contacted me and desired a visit. Looking back, I often think that I should have spent the rest of my days in the islands of the Caribbean preaching the gospel and seeking to help the saints. However, the work at home also burdened me and I took it to be the mind of the Lord that my main work would be in Northern Ireland and to visit the islands as the Lord would lead.

On my third trip, I brought my wife Betsy with me. Though I say it myself, Betsy was a charming girl that could mix with anyone. She took to the people of Barbados. She got to know so many by name and the young sisters flocked round her every time we arrived at meetings. From that visit on, I always had to have Betsy with me. I do not think the saints would have allowed me to come without her. I got many invitations to dine with the believers in their homes, but it was Betsy they really wanted. Many of the folk took us out to the most interesting and expensive restaurants. Even the mosquitoes were delighted to greet her! They kept coming to her day by day. Betsy had a terrible time with the many bites. We had to burn the coils in the bedroom each night. We tried rubs and suchlike, but all was of little help. The assemblies ran a home in Bridgetown for the older saints who could not care for themselves. I used to visit often to pass a word of encouragement to them from the Scriptures. On one particular visit, a nice little lady spoke to my wife about the many bites on her legs and arms.

She recommended her to get citronella from the chemist and put it on her arms and legs. If she did this, not a mosquito would come within four feet of her because of the aroma. Now this turned out to be true. She had great peace, but it kept some people at distance from her as well!

I remember we arrived at the hall quite early for a meeting. Two little sisters with their straw hats on their heads sat near the platform so as to hear the speaker better. One said to the other in what was supposed to be a whisper, "Sister Jennings is in the hall". "I know", said the other. "I can smell her!" Almost every day, young and old sisters in the Lord came to visit sister Jennings. She helped quite a number with their problems. They also invited her some mornings to teach the sisters how to bake; especially soda bread and such like. Actually, I could have told them much better as I was a baker to trade before I left this occupation to preach the gospel full time. However, the fellowship was great for my wife and the sisters in the Lord as well.

I must say, having my wife with me in Barbados was used of the Lord for me to know in a more personal way the beloved saints in the Lord. A young couple became her close friends. This brother and sister in Christ were married the previous year when I was there on my own. Now, cricket is a big thing in the West Indies, and this girl was tremendous at the game. The young believers in the assemblies often took lots of children to the beach on Saturday morning or afternoon. They had a picnic and some Bible lessons then a game of cricket. Once this girl was batting, there was no hope of ever getting her out. She had always to retire from the game to give others a chance to play. However, cricket brought her an admirer, a lovely young brother, and eventually they were married. I was invited to the wedding. Such a display! The wedding party was fabulous, with the bride and groom, the best man, bridesmaid, then another three men linked with another three girls. If I remember right there was a little boy and girl as well. All were dressed in the very best. A brother, Monroe

Franklin, conducted the ceremony. He had the responsibility for all the weddings among the believers. He was the marrying man and yet he was never married himself. He told me that some were critical of him saying he ought not to take weddings because he was single. I asked him whether he ever took a funeral. "Quite a lot", he told me. I said, "Tell such people, 'I take funerals although I was never dead at the time.'" Everyone was invited to the wedding; the hall was packed to capacity and many were standing outside. Everyone was dressed in the very best that money could buy. The wedding took place at 2p.m. and it was about an hour and a half later that all who wanted to go to the reception departed to a certain beach. A large area of the beach was ringed off with poles and floodlights which came on when the darkness fell. First, there were speeches. There were many of them and I was getting hungry. Each speech lasted about twenty minutes or more. Everyone was having a whale of a time for some of the speeches were amusing and sometimes very funny. The darkness fell and still the speeches went on. Besides being hungry, I was also getting very tired. So, at about 9.30p.m. I could stand it no more and a brother took me home to Nell's house. I was glad to get to bed as the next day was Lord's Day and I had a busy day ahead.

The thing I remember most was the wedding cake. Actually, there were five cakes with little ladders joining cake to cake. All adorned with little brides and grooms and other things of that nature. I took a photo of the cake, as that was part of my trade in the past, making and decorating wedding cakes.

As I said, the young couple became very dear friends to us. Sometime after the wedding when I was there with my wife, they asked us to meet them for a picnic and - Could we help them with a problem in their marriage? We met them in fear and trembling; we did not feel we had the experience to deal with problems in marriage. The young couple took us to a lovely park and they had enough food for twenty people. There were about four baskets containing lovely sandwiches and cakes and so forth. After the meal, I thought we would get this over with and I asked them what the problem in their marriage was. The girl did the speaking, the problem was – Should a couple pray together or individually and should the wife pray in the presence of her husband? This was so different from what we expected and I was able to give them light on this subject. After that we had a merry time together. This is one little episode that sticks in my mind to this day.

The twelve assembles on the island worked together in a most spiritual way. They had quarterly meetings for a day of prayer and ministry. Each assembly took it in turn to arrange this meeting. Generally, the morning was given to prayer, the afternoon to a Bible Reading and the evening was given to ministry. I conducted many of these Bible Readings over the years and the exchange of thought was of a very intelligent manner. It appeared also that about every two or three months they had an overseers' meeting. About two elders from each meeting would gather together to encourage each other and plan various meetings, and whilst they did not interfere with each other's problems, it helped to keep harmony and also share the news from the different assemblies such as meetings they had planned. This was a help to each assembly and I think something like this goes on to the present day.

I must close this section with a few remarks on the ministry meetings that made my visit a delight indeed.

I remember one night I was speaking on the country side of Barbados, the coast that faces the Atlantic. Another brother and I arrived about ten minutes before the time and there was only one brother present. I said, "Where are the people?" He explained that very few folk in the village had clocks. They knew to come to the meeting when they heard the singing. The three of us began to sing. Within about three minutes, people began to come into the building. About half the seats were taken when I commenced the meeting. I had just prayed and was about to read the Scriptures when the lights went out. Now lighting in the streets had not come to the villages of Barbados. I just carried on; I had memorized the

Airy Hill Gospel Hall, Barbados

passage that I was reading and was able to repeat it in the dark. Also, I did not need any notes for that particular subject and so just preached on, light or no light. I heard a little shuffle at times while I spoke. After about half an hour, the light came on again and the hall was full of smiling faces from the front of the hall to the back with many standing. In the dark I could not see the black faces of the dear people coming into the meeting, but the light revealed all. This is a great lesson and the Scriptures teach this - the things done in the darkness shall be revealed by the light.

Another amusing thing happened at an assembly called Stream, which is situated along the coast. The building was large with a very high ceiling. The podium was also very high. The carpenter who made it must have been very tall. When I stood before it and put my Bible on the top it was just level with my forehead. To overcome this, the brethren placed a box that the preacher could stand on to give his address. Now in this particular meeting the box had disappeared. Actually some sister had borrowed it to reach something in the kitchen and had forgotten to put the box back again. This was a very special meeting and the large hall was full.

Now the brother that gave out the opening hymn and welcomed the people stood behind the podium and was heard but not seen. People were looking around wondering where the voice was coming from. Every head was turning right and left and behind and failed to see the speaker. To them he was certainly not on the platform. They were not aware of the absent box! When the time came for me to speak, I stepped aside from the podium and spoke from there. It was I who discovered the box in the kitchen when I went there for a drink of cold water after the meeting.

Helpful Believers

Now I must write a few words about some of the distinguished and spiritual brethren of Barbados. Men I soon got to know and love. I admired their wisdom and discernment in many ways.

First there was a brother called Fred Ashby. Every brother and sister looked up to him. He had a wonderful grasp of Scripture and the ability to teach the same. His life commended his teaching. He was gentle yet firm when error arose from time to time in Dayrells Road, of which he was an overseer, and in other assemblies as well. I remember on one occasion I was speaking over a few nights in Dayrells Road and the interest and numbers were delightful. My wife and I came in by the side door about ten minutes before the time of the meeting. To my horror, a Pentecostal woman was on the platform speaking. She just got up from her seat halfway down the hall and went up the steps onto the platform uninvited. The sisters in the meeting were very ashamed of this deed done by a woman. They knew a woman's place in the gatherings of the saints. Some brethren commanded her to come down, all of whom she ignored. I thought, I will get up and start the meeting over her head and give out an opening hymn and the singing would silence her. The great volume of the singing would overpower her. However, Fred Ashby entered the hall, stood at the platform and cried, "In the Name of the Lord Jesus, come down from the platform". He said this twice and the woman shut her mouth and came down from the platform and left the building. I admired the spiritual power in the man.

Elder from a Barbados Assembly

He was married a second time to a wonderful sister from Canada whose name was Mazina. This sister was a tremendous help to Fred in all that he sought to do for the Lord and His people. She nursed brother Ashby in his final illness right to the day on which he was called home to the glory. I will always remember Fred Ashby. He was greatly missed. Now, Fred had a brother who was a missionary in Anguilla, a very small island. Later, on another visit, I was invited to Anguilla and met this man who was a giant in the faith, William Ashby. I will write of him later when I get to Anguilla in this book.

Another great brother was Horace Hoyt. He is the brother that invited me to my first meeting in Barbados when he met us at the KFC. He ran a little travel agency and was a leading brother in the Fitz village assembly. Hoyt had a great sense of humour and yet was very wise in all he did and said. His wife was a very charming woman, the daughter of a minister in one of the churches of Barbados. She was very good looking and folk just took to her to such a degree that she could almost get away with anything. One occasion I remember: she and her husband took me to the airport as I was travelling to another island at the time. A very long queue was leading up to the check-in desk. My flight was going in about twenty minutes and I thought I would miss the plane. Evelyn just went along the queue with me following. She charmed everybody with a smile until we got to the desk and I checked in before anyone else. Everybody just smiled at her. She charmed both men and women with her genial way. They often took me for a meal or picnic and to most interesting places of historic legends on the island. Alas, he too is with the Lord. I missed him the times I visited the island after that.

Monroe Franklin is another excellent brother. He took all the weddings in Barbados, as I have written earlier in this book. He was an elder in Crompton Street, the assembly with the very large building where I had the meeting on my first visit. He had a wonderful testimony with all he came in contact. Wisdom and discernment were his chief qualities; many looked up to him when problems arose. Brother Monroe was always smiling and delightful to talk to. Often he would invite me to meet him for lunch in the Cave Shepherd apartment store in Bridgetown. He could give a good word of ministry and chaired many of the conferences. A very capable helpful brother is Monroe Franklin. As far as I know, he is still living and continuing in the Lord.

There was an older brother called Bostic. He too was looked up to by all the assemblies. He owned a lot of property which he let out. He was a well-to-do brother, but down to earth at the same time. He loved when I visited Barbados. He always said to me, "Welcome home". Actually, he wanted me to go and live on the island and he offered me a rent-free house if I would do so. He attended every meeting where I was speaking and encouraged me with words of cheer. His wife had beautiful dark hair right down her back. They invited me for dinner one day. I arrived and was sure I was at the right address. This little lady came to the door. She had short grey hair. I said, "Sorry, I am at the wrong address". Then the woman said to me, "You are at the right address. I am

Mrs. Bostic but I do not have my wig on!" We had a lovely meal together. Brother Bostic and his dear wife are now also gone home to the glory.

Most of the older women in the West Indies wear wigs; this is a common thing to do. I remember being in another house with an older brother who was very tall and his wife were very small. I said, "I would like a photo of you" and she hurried to find her wig before I took the picture. Even younger sisters in the meeting wore wigs. These were so expertly made that one could not tell. I admired the hair of a very friendly good-looking sister and while dining in their home I remarked that she had lovely hair. She pulled it off and said, "Yes, this is one of my wigs!"

Another dear brother I will always remember - beloved brother Cyril Murray and his wife Mildred. He was born in Barbados and as a young man had emigrated to the States and lived in New York. In due course, he and his dear wife were commended by the black assemblies of New York City to preach the gospel in Barbados. He had a large American car that was sent to him from New York and he seemed to be very well supported by the dear believers of the New York assemblies. I never heard the dear brother preach. I met him for the first time in Cherry Grove where I took my first meeting in coming to Barbados. The work brother Murray did was tremendous. I think he did the work of three men. He was always there to help the believers no matter what assembly they belonged to. He took the older Christians to the doctors and the hospital for their treatment, and then waited to take them home again.

He visited everyone that was sick. He spoke at and helped with funerals. He did messages and shopping for the older saints who were in the retirement home. He also helped very much the smaller assemblies. He just never seemed to stop. He became a dear friend to me. He said he loved me because I helped the assemblies. He had me in his house several times for a meal. His wife was a very cheerful little lady, but full of wisdom at the same time. Very often this dear sister Mildred pushed an envelope into my pocket that contained a precious gift in the Lord. I remember the time an English brother who was a missionary in St. Kitts came for a visit to Barbados. He did this from time to time. He was a good friend of brother Murray. One morning, brother Murray took the English brother, Nell, my wife and me and another little clergyman to lunch in a lovely place called Sam Lord's Castle. I learned later that this was one of the most expensive places to lunch. However, it was worth it. The food was delicious and plentiful and the service was without fault. This turned out to be a happy memory for all of us. We had a wonderful time of delightful fellowship together. Mr. Murray paid for the lot of us. How kind of him just to give each one of us a treat. On a later occasion, I took my wife to Sam Lord's for a meal and when I saw the prices I decided to dine somewhere else! As for the little clergyman, he came from England every year and stayed for a month with Nell. He was a single gentleman and full of humour and told us delightful stories of his experiences as a minister of a large church in England. He had the ability to keep us all amused with his fund of stories. We had such a wonderful time at Sam Lord's Castle that I often recall it to this day.

I saw another side to brother Murray one day. He guarded the assemblies. If anyone was invited to take meetings in Barbados and he knew the invited speaker had a reputation for dividing or hindering the assemblies in any way, he made sure that the invitation was withdrawn. He guarded the assemblies this way. I actually heard him in very strong language demand that one such should be cancelled. Mr. Murray was zealous for the assemblies and sought to see to it that they had as little trouble as possible.

Mr. Murray passed away when I was at home in Northern Ireland. The next time I was there I went to see his grave and stood there for a long time remembering this dear brother. He was always willing to take a lower place in service to the saints in love. He was missed by so many for all his deeds of kindness. I do not think anyone could have taken his place. I went to see Mildred his wife and she passed on to me one of his books, which I treasure. He did not have many books - he was a labourer rather than a student. He has gone to glory and his works do follow him. In his life, he put the Lord and the need of the believers before himself. A very godly and Scriptural way to live, as was taught by the Lord Jesus. To me he was a great man of God, not so much on the platform but behind the scenes for the glory of God and the blessing of the believers. His life so lived was an example to all who knew him.

Another one of the dear saints that I appreciated very much was a gentleman named McPherson. He was older than me but a down-to-earth and energetic man. He attended most of the meetings I spoke at. He had a wonderful thirst for the Word. I do not remember if he drove a car but he always accompanied those who collected me for a meeting. I remember one night after the meeting he and another brother left me at Nell's house where I was staying. Nell was not at home - this was very rare - and so the door was locked. I saw that some of the windows were open for air as is the case with most if not all the houses on the island. Most windows were narrow or had netting on the inside to keep burglars from having an easy entrance to the house. The house that Nell lived in was an old colonial building, all on one floor but the building was on a sort of stilt frame with a flight of steps leading up to the front door and the windows were therefore quite high. Brother McPherson indicated that I stand on his shoulders, reach a window and climb into the house. Such a struggle I had getting onto the shoulders of this dear brother. He almost buckled under my weight, but the other brother who was our driver that night helped him. He held McPherson while he held me. I thought of the occasion when the arms of Moses were upheld by Aaron and Hur! After quite a struggle of heaving and lifting and grunting I got a grip on the window sill and entered the house. I then went to the hall and opened the door and said "Good night" to them and off they went. I often look back to this simple thing with great amusement. We acted like a couple of youngsters rather than full-grown men. I remember that I slept well that night, maybe the physical effort made me tired. Every time I came to Barbados for gospel or ministry, brother McPherson was my companion. We had wonderful times together discussing the ministry after every meeting.

On one of my later visits, I got the news that brother McPherson had just passed away. He had gone home. I was so sorry; I felt the loss very keenly. The funeral was on Saturday, two days after I arrived.

I have mentioned in this book that funerals were special occasions in the West Indies, more-so in Barbados. The friends and family all gathered together in a very large building. There must have been several hundred present. The funerals in Barbados use caskets similar to the States and Canada. The casket was at the front of the hall, just before the platform, and was open. There was a door to the left of the casket and every one entered by this door, then approached the casket and bowed before it and then was led to a seat. The ceremony started with the singing of about six hymns. The volume was terrific and the harmony out of this world. Many a tear was shed during that singing. After the tributes by his sons and others, the message was given by brother Lionel Weeks who always spoke with true feelings at such times. I did not go to the grave but went back to Nell's house where I again was staying. How I missed the company of that dear brother McPherson both then and in the later visits to the island.

Another beloved brother comes very much to the fore in my mind. He was the leading brother in the small assembly in Airy Hill. His name slips me at the moment. He was not so much a platform man but served the saints in collecting them and driving them to the meetings. He had a little van that served this purpose. It had covered over 200,000 miles and that is another experience that I will write of further in this book.

There was a brother in the Fairview assembly named Franklin Brown. He was an elder in the assembly and also was called upon for advice from the brethren of some of the other assemblies. Franklin and his wife became close friends with Betsy and me. They often took us out for lunch and also sometimes entertained us in their own lovely home. The wife of Franklin was very humorous. She was good in a company, a very pretty and funny person. Sometimes the Christians lent me a car for the time I was there. This proved very useful. On one occasion, I took brother Brown and his wife home after the meeting. Then I began to drive off and the wife of Franklin shouted, "Stop, stop! There is something moving at the side of your car". I stopped in a sort of fear. "Oh", she said, "it is the wheel of your car going round!" I still think often of this happy pair.

Two of my closest friends in Barbados I must now write about, because they helped me greatly in the work. This was a Maggie Fletcher and her brother Robert, known as Bobby. They were brought up in the Exclusive assemblies which at one time were very strong in Barbados with about twenty halls. The chief speakers among the Exclusives often visited these meetings from time to time. One in particular was the well-known teacher named Jim Taylor senior. He visited the island almost every year and stayed for a few months taking Bible Readings and ministering the Word. Maggie and Bobby were brought up as children in this atmosphere. However, when James Taylor junior became the leading man within the Exclusives, his teaching did dreadful harm to that group of assemblies.

Especially in Barbados this canker was seen. The idea of not eating with one who was not a member of their group went to great extremes. I came across many of these dear true believers whose lives had been terribly disrupted by their doctrine. I remember visiting a dear brother on his death bed and none of his family would visit him. They separated totally from him over the years because he had left the fellowship because of this teaching. He died and not one of his family or friends attended his funeral. A few neighbours and a few Christians from other places were at the funeral. Now this is contrary to the custom in Barbados, where a funeral is a big thing and attended by hundreds of folk who maybe just heard of the person. They also dress up for the occasion. The ladies clothed with the latest fashion as if they were going to a wedding instead of a funeral. The men also with suits, complete with a waistcoat and tie with shining shoes. I remember driving through a village and the streets were lined with people and hundreds of children in their school uniforms. I stopped and asked a little girl why the crowd of people were there. She answered me and explained that it was a funeral. I asked her who the person was who was dead. She just said to me, "I don't know". Well, this dear Exclusive man in his death was so different. I remember talking to a sister and her children in the street one day and a woman passed by. The sister said to me, "That was my mother that passed by. She is one of the old Exclusive group and will no longer acknowledge me or my family". The outcome of all this was that the Exclusive meetings on the island broke up. Many kept to their teaching but went nowhere as far as a gathering of the saints is concerned. Maggie Fletcher eventually came into our assemblies; Bobby came to the meeting at times but was never in fellowship until his life was nearly finished. Now Maggie was a very close friend of Nell and through her we came to know Maggie.

She was a wonderful person, a keen believer and very well taught in the Word. An excellent cook and housekeeper, she lived in a lovely home. Maggie was well thought of on the island not only by the white people but by the black folk as well. I remember on one of my visits with my wife, Maggie hired a large house on the shore and the four of us including Nell had a wonderful break in a lovely home right on the shore. I had a swim most mornings and enjoyed the break although I always had a meeting to take each evening somewhere on the island. The brethren came and collected me for the meeting and brought me back again. I remember one warm but stormy morning the waves were very high as they rolled and crashed on the shore. I would judge that the waves were about ten to twelve feet high as we were on the Atlantic side of the island. Red flags warning of the danger to swimmers were stuck in the sand about every few hundred feet apart. Sally McCune said she was going for a swim. I said, "You dare not do so. Look at the red flags of warning". Sally was a very determined woman who did her own thing no matter what. At times this was good, but this time it was a foolish thing to do. However, she had made up her mind and off she went. I changed into bathing trunks and went with her, but not to swim. Sally stepped into a wave that was on its way out and paddled at the edge of the turbulent water. Then a huge wave came in and crashed down on Sally. She was tumbled round and round like a towel in a washing machine. Sometimes her knees would appear then her head then her feet. If it had not been so serious, one could have laughed at her circling round in the raging water. The water receded and Sally was on her knees, but I could see another huge wave rolling in. I ran and caught her by the arms and literally trailed her from the water onto the dry shore. When I told her how foolish it was to go into the huge waves, she just answered, "It was very refreshing". Maggie became a very dear friend to my wife and me. She was so good and wise and often kept us in her lovely well-ordered home. I always especially enjoyed the cooking at these times. Her bread-and-butter pudding was the best I ever tasted.

Now Bobby had a brother who was a very rich man. He owned a beautiful mansion in Barbados. In later life he had trouble with his skin especially on his face and the sunshine of the West Indies made the matter worse. He also had another home in Canada, so he stayed mostly in Canada and when the snow season started, he came to the sunshine in Barbados for a month or two each year. Most of the time his lovely house in Barbados was left unoccupied. This gentleman then offered the house to me and my wife on one of our visits. Sally McCune also stayed with us. It was delightful to rise in the morning and to look over the lovely lawns and to take one's breakfast in such a well laid out kitchen with every modern device to aid the cooking. I did not have to care for the lawns as a boy was appointed to come every week to cut them. I was surprised that a swimming pool was absent in the grounds of this house as it was the norm in most similar houses. However, there was a large parrot in a very large cage just at the back door. The parrot did not like me. Every time I passed by, he got into a terrible state and yelled and roared at me. When Betsy or Sally passed, he just jumped with joy and delight. It was necessary to pass him as one went out of the kitchen to the garden. As soon as the bird saw me, he started his shouting and roaring. Most mornings I stood for a moment at his cage and talked to him and he shouted more and more. He then flapped his wings in anger and glared at me with his piercing eyes. When I walked away, he immediately became quiet. At times I just popped out for a minute just to hear him shout and scream. It was all very amusing to me. Sometimes I would shout back and this made him all the madder. I have no idea why the parrot disliked me so much.

I thought Maggie would have stayed with us even for a few days as there was plenty of room in the house. She thought it necessary to stay in her own home because house burglary was very common on the islands.

During our stay in that great house, Robert Graham with his wife came to stay for a length of time during one of their visits to Barbados. Robert was a good help to the meetings and he with his wife were very much loved and appreciated by all. Well, on that occasion the Grahams also stayed with us in the lovely palatial house. We used to sit up late together and chat, that is apart from Sally who was always early to bed and early to rise.

One morning, Sally McCune spoke to us while we were at breakfast, saying she did not like her bedroom. It was sort of dark. There was a much larger bedroom across the hall from her. However, this room was full of furniture, books and the belongings of some missionaries from the States who worked with children and were on furlough at that time. The room was neatly packed right from floor to ceiling from back to the entrance door. It would have been difficult to push another article inside. Sally was insistent that this was the room for her. Robert and I had the task of moving all the furniture and other items to the large garage in the grounds of the house. Now the garage was quite a distance from the house. The task took the whole afternoon. We made innumerable trips to and fro carrying heavy furniture, books and toys, clothes, kitchen utensils and many other things. When finished, we were completely exhausted and covered in sweat. After a shower and some food, we began to recover. The next morning at breakfast, Sally came into the kitchen and I knew by the look of her face something was wrong. "Well", I said, "did you sleep well?" "No", she said, "that side of the house is too near the road and a man passing by looked in at my window". We all said that the passers-by could see nothing as it was dark inside and light outside. Besides, there was a light covering on the window. All that was not good enough. She must have her own room back again! So we spent the morning moving all her things from the large room to the room she had at the first. We thought also that it would be better to restore the belongings of the missionary couple from the garage to the room, which thing we did, another day of toil and sweat. We had intended to do that at the end of our visit anyway, so the task was done. Sally then was quite content with her room. I often thought that Sally just liked to make people work, to keep them busy!

On another occasion when my wife was with me in Barbados, I was booked for three nights each in two halls near the district of Bathsheba on the Atlantic side of the island. The local people made two words to name this place, Bath – Sheba; the emphasis was on the word "Bath". Now there was a dear white sister in the Ebenezer assembly who owned a house on the beach near

Bathsheba. The house was called Bit by Bit, the house alongside it was called Piece by Piece and the next house Box by Box, and so forth. The reason for such names occurred because to begin with there were only a few huts there. People bought them and added another room. Sometime later another room was added to the house and so on. The houses were quite large and very expensive to buy. This dear sister let us have Bit by Bit for the week I was speaking on that side of the island. I just loved being there. It was the happiest time of all the experiences I had in Barbados. I think of this often to this present day.

The beach in front of the house stretched for several miles. The waves were always crashing upon the shore. I went to bed each night with the sound of the wind and the surf of the huge waves. I kept the window of the room open at night to enjoy the refreshing cool air. There was a veranda around all the front of the house and we took our breakfast on that veranda each morning. There were a lot of blackbirds about, not as big as the blackbirds at home, actually quite small. Betsy my wife made the mistake of leaving food for them one morning. When we went to take our breakfast the next morning, the rail around the veranda was completely filled with birds waiting for their breakfast! Every inch of the rail was covered and they were all chirping. It took me a long time to chase them away; they keep coming back looking and shouting for their breakfast. My wife never fed them again for the rest of the week. These birds were a little smaller than a pigeon and it appeared that they did not sing but let out a soft tweet every few seconds or so. A number of them could create quite a racket.

My wife was much loved by the people. She was kind to all and excellent with all sorts of children. Betsy was a very sincere Christian and would always stand for the truth no matter the cost. We used to go to the beach most mornings when we stayed with Nell. Her home was only five minutes from the shore.

My wife splashed at the edge of the water while I went into the waves for a swim. We then walked along the beach for about ten minutes or so. This is what most people did after their swim. Another man also walked the beach after his swim and we became very friendly with him. He had a position quite high up in the government and was quite a gentleman in his manner and demeanour. He especially took to us when he heard we came from Northern Ireland. He had a brother who was a doctor and his practice was in Belfast. In one of our conversations with him we informed him that we were going home to Ireland in a few days. He told us quite sincerely that he would miss us. Then he asked us if we would deliver a gift from him to his brother in Belfast and we agreed to do so. Now we thought the gift would be a flying fish that Barbados is famous for, wrapped up very nicely for visitors to take home with them. These were prepared by a very good firm on the island. However, the next day the man called with Nell and left us a bottle of rum to take to his brother. We did not expect this and Sally and Nell said we should just leave it behind. My wife Betsy, however, disagreed. She said that we had to let the man know that we could not deliver this potent rum to anyone anywhere. So Betsy called him on the phone and I was standing beside her. She greeted the gentleman and said in nice gentle way that we were Christians. We had come to the Island to help Christians and therefore it would be error on our part to carry rum in our belongings. Betsy also added that we preached to the young people of the island, warning them of the danger of drinking rum etc. We would then be hypocrites if we were to deliver the same as a gift. The man was disappointed in us but just said in a grumpy way that he would come and collected the rum. The next day he did so when we were out. The following morning, which was our last, we went for our walk up and down the beach. We met him but he walked on the other side and turned his head away from us. Such was my wife. She was a very sincere Christian and sought to maintain the testimony unto the Lord Jesus.

Now I must refer again to the brother who drove the van in the Airy Hill assembly. This dear brother spent much time each week endeavouring to keep the old van on the road. It was always giving trouble and I saw the need for a new van. I had just written a book on the Revelation and named it, "Alpha and Omega", before I left home to come to Barbados. On arrival again in Belfast I began to sell this book and in a little time I had made about three thousand pounds profit. I decided to put this money towards a new van for the Airy Hill assembly. In some way that I do not know, the Lord's Work Trust heard of this and they put a large sum of money to the cause. I then had the money to purchase a new van. I passed this money to the brother in Airy Hill and the brethren started putting all in motion. The van was purchased in New York and the black assemblies there paid for its delivery to the dear brother in Barbados. The new van seated about twenty people and was beautifully painted with Airy Hill Gospel Hall on each side. Now no one drove the carrier van except this particular brother. He washed it every day because the salt in the air of the islands rusts a motor vehicle very quickly if not washed often. He alone cared for and maintained the carrier. As far as I know the van is still in service to the saints. When meetings were being conducted anywhere on the island, the van made about three or four trips and brought over sixty people to that particular meeting. The carrier van was a gift from God and a rich blessing to the beloved saints of the island.

Speaking of writing books, it never occurred in my mind to write a book until I had an experience on a particular visit to the United States. I shared a conference with a dear brother from Canada named Daniel Smith. He was a lovely kind of man, the sort that would not sleep if he knew he had offended anyone. I took to him very quickly and enjoyed his ministry very much. He gave very suitable words of encouragement and comfort. After the meeting, both of us were invited to the home of the leading man in the assembly where the conference was held. I had spoken on Isaac and his place in the New Testament. This little man was very much taken up with what I said; to him it was fresh and helpful. Then he asked me if I had ever written a book. I answered that it never entered my mind to do so. He advised me that the next time I took a series on some part of Scripture that I should write a book on it; each morning seeking to write the ministry of the previous night while it was fresh in my mind.

Brother Smith was a real gentleman and a loving Christian. He lived in British Columbia in Canada and had been in China for some years as a missionary. He fled that country when trouble started and settled in Canada. He had never learnt to drive a car. He just went on a tour of assemblies to help with the ministry and travelled about in the Greyhound buses. Now the journeys of these buses can be very long and tiring, but he put in the time with a typewriter on his knee writing devotional books and then he sold them as he went from place to place. I marvel that he found something interesting in what I said to encourage me to write a book. No one had ever suggested that I do such a thing as to write a book. It so happened that when in Barbados on another visit I stayed with Sally McCune. She had retired for a time from the work in Dominica and rented a house in Barbados. She was beginning to feel her age and sought to be among friends that could take care for her if she took ill. The house she lived in was called Train-view. Why this was I will never know, as railways and trains were unknown on the islands. There was a beautiful view of the sea and a quaint little harbour. I had a week's ministry before me in one of the halls and had an exercise to speak on Noah for the five nights. I then remembered the encouragement of brother Smith, the bus man, and decided to write about Noah. My plan was to speak at night and the next morning to write down all that I had said about the character of Noah - and this I did. I spoke each evening to a large company and then early in the morning I sat on a chair on the veranda of Train-view and wrote out the message of the ministry in longhand. I spent a little over two hours each morning in this way and then had my breakfast with Sally.

She was an early riser each day and spent the early morning writing letters and later had her breakfast. So there was I sitting and writing with a lovely view of the sea and Sally was sitting writing in her kitchen with a view of the walls. Then we had breakfast together. As I wrote each morning about Noah other points came into my mind and so I continued writing until the book was finished.

Soon after this, I was on a visit to the U.S.A. and I told this to a brother who suggested he keep the manuscript and he would type it out for me. At that time I did not possess a computer. Such things were just appearing on the scene at that time. Over time the brother in America had little time to type the book and after some months it was returned to me. By that time I had purchased one of the early computers.

An amusing story comes out of this. Some of the saints in Northern Ireland and elsewhere frowned on computers. They were the work of the devil, some said. At that time I was in a series of gospel meetings with brother Jim Flanigan.

He also worked with a computer in those early days. We were in a little sister's house for tea before the meeting one night and she told of a preacher who had a computer. "Terrible", she said, "he ought not to be on a platform. A man with the Word in his hand and a computer in his house, how carnal". Jim and I looked at each other with a smile. We knew the brother she named, an excellent teacher of the Word. Now as both of us had computers, we just smiled and said nothing. Things have wonderfully changed since that time. I was able to type the book myself and wondered what I would do with the manuscript. Then I got a phone call from John Ritchie, the Christian publishers. They informed me that they had heard I was writing a book on Noah. I affirmed that was so and they said they would publish the book. In due time, Noah appeared on the bookshelves of Christian book shops and sold very well. Since that time I have written several other books, but it all started with brother Smith and Barbados. I often just think of the lovely mornings I just sat on a most comfortable chair with the sea before me, a pen in my hand and some paper on my knee. That is how it all began.

On about my third visit to Barbados I saw a keen interest in the gospel. Several of the brethren were able ministers of the gospel and each assembly had a short series in the gospel from time to time. I spoke to the chief brethren about the use of a tent for gospel preaching, pointing out that a tent would be more attractive to encourage people to come in to meetings rather than the halls. I informed them that Trinidad and other islands in the Caribbean made use of tents for the spread of the gospel. The brethren told me that they had often thought of it and some had suggested this in the past. I told them to consider this and to pray concerning a gospel tent. After some weeks I was in the homeland again. Some assemblies in Northern Ireland often invited me for a report of the work in the West Indies. I was invited to the Kells assembly in Co. Antrim for a report and I happened to mention a tent for the work in Barbados. To my surprise, a few days later I received from the brethren in Kells a gift of 1000 pounds towards a tent for the spread of the gospel in the lovely sunny island of Barbados. A few days later a brother from another assembly approached me and informed me that he heard about the exercise of a tent for the gospel in the West Indies. I told him that was so and he passed on to me a cheque for another 1000 pounds. In a few days the Lord had turned up 2000 pounds towards a tent and I got on the phone with brother Monroe Franklin and informed him of this. I told him if the brethren decided on a tent I would forward this money and if not I would give it back to the donors.

Monroe informed me that he would gather the chief men among the brethren together that very night to consider this project. The following evening Monroe phoned me and informed me that there was complete harmony among the brethren and to send the money right away. I went to the little Ulster Bank the next day in the High Street, Bangor; I was living in Bangor at that time. I asked them what the cost would be to send the 2000 pounds to Barbados. "What is this money for?", the bank assistant asked me. I told her this was towards a tent for gospel work on the island.

She then informed me that there would not be any charge as this would come under charity work. Wonderful, the money was with the brethren in Barbados that very day. Things soon began to move. The brethren ordered the tent from New York, from a firm that specialised in making tents. The brethren in the New York assemblies then paid the difference between the 2000 pounds and the price of the tent. They also paid for the transport of the tent to Barbados. In due course the tent arrived.

The brethren of all twelve assemblies got together to consider the working of the tent. The decision was unanimous that the tent would be erected twice a year and shared round the twelve assemblies in turn. This meant that two districts would be covered each year and all twelve halls would be covered every six years.

It was also arranged that the hall in Airy Hill would house the tent and poles when not in use. This assembly had a very large room at the back of their hall which would preserve the tent from dampness and other things. As far as I know the tent is still in operation and the sharing of the same by each assembly.

I had the privilege of having a series in the gospel in the said tent about three years after it first arrived.

The tent was constructed in broad stripes of red and white for the roof. This made it very attractive. The sides were also in the same way with the red and white stripes. Generally speaking, the sides were only put up when it was raining. The tent was perfectly fireproof. There was very good seating arrangement for about three hundred people. The meetings were always in the evenings when the folk were free of their work etc. Now the darkness falls upon Barbados about 6 p.m. in the winter and 6.30 p.m. in the summer, as far as I remember. The meeting then took place an hour after darkness but the brethren had a wonderful set of lighting. The tent was lit up as if in daylight.

The sides of the tent being rolled up meant that people coming could do so in any direction and this helped strangers to attend. Others stood outside the tent and could hear perfectly. Hymnbooks were not needed as the brethren were experts in PowerPoint and such things. The words of the hymn appeared on a very large screen. Each night a different assembly chaired the meeting. About three or four brethren did this each night. One would lead the singing which lasted about half an hour. One would pray and another make announcements and so on. The tent was full to capacity each night as many Pentecostal folk also attended. A good number were present each night who were strangers to the grace we know in Christ. The Lord added the blessing. Over the years the tent has been erected in many different places in Barbados and many people have trusted the Lord Jesus for salvation. They went on to be a light and salt to all among the people of their district.

The last night of the tent was a special and wonderful occasion. The young people had the job of taking down the tent and putting it on a large truck to transport it to the store in Airy Hill. About fifty young believers sang as they worked at dismantling the tent. Each large section was spread upon the ground and then dried with cloths on both sides. This was necessary, as the tent gathered much moisture and salt during the time it was used. If stored without this cleansing the tent would rot and become mouldy during the time of storage. Now this was all done during the darkness of the evening. Light for the task came from the cars of the believers. They circled the area of the tent with the lights of each car shining on the work. Almost everyone waited after the meeting for the taking down of the tent. The bright lights and the singing of so many young people toiling to clean the tent turned out to be a happy experience. When the truck was fully loaded and had gone on its way, all the young people set out for donuts and coffee in one of the large coffee restaurants in the city. I think it was very late by the time the folk then got to their beds for the night. Now this all took place after a series in the tent was over. While all supported the meetings, the young people made the final night something to look forward to.

During the third trip I had to Barbados, quite a number of young brethren took a keen interest in learning the Scriptures. They studied as individuals and sometimes two or three would study together and Bible Readings became very popular. Some of the leading brethren sought to help them and decided to ask me to have a sort of gathering and speak of methods of approaching the Scriptures. Now this is something I had taken an interest in over the years. I had read about different methods of Bible study and with some of them I totally disagreed. I found some good methods in the writings of others that were quite helpful. I finally had worked out a plan that covered all the New Testament in one year and a method of keeping notes concerning the same. Therefore, a meeting was arranged for a Saturday evening and Nell was willing that the meeting would take place in her spacious home. The brethren at that time had the mind that the hall was for assembly meetings only, but this gathering especially concerned the young brethren. Nell had an enormous sitting room which was most suitable for the occasion. I expected a number short of twenty but the number that turned up was almost double that. So I sat down facing all these young believers of Barbados, a few interested sisters were among the eager young brethren. I spoke for about a half hour on the rich blessing to oneself and to others that a working knowledge of the Scriptures reaped. Then I spoke about different methods that Scofield and others had recommended. I then outlined my own method and left the rest of the time to questions and suggestions. We had a wonderful time. I knew that some of these dear brethren were growing to be the young men that John wrote about in 1 John 2 verse 14: "I have written unto you, young men, because ye are strong and the word of God abideth in you, and ye have overcome the wicked one". Some of the young men in the Nell's house that night later became the overseers in some of the assemblies. Others developed very well in the Word and became a great help to the believers. I think of one brother in particular. He was in the police and keenly followed every meeting I spoke at in Barbados. He made it a habit to record the ministry and then listened to the recording many times until he had got all into his mind. The name of this brother is Lionel Weeks. Later, he left the police and with the fellowship of the brethren gave himself to the work of the Lord. Since then he has been a wonderful help to the assemblies in Barbados and to other islands as well. He has been invited further abroad to the assemblies in Canada and other places. He is a sound preacher of the gospel and a tremendous help in the ministry. The meeting that Saturday night in the house of Nell was blessed of the Lord.

Another occasion I remember very well is a one-off conference in Crompton Street assembly, the one that Monroe Franklin attended. The special conference was in remembrance of the planting of the assembly fifty years earlier. At that time there was an English brother who laboured in Jamaica called Harold Wildish. He had been invited for meetings in Bridgetown. He was an excellent preacher of the gospel and the Lord blessed his labours abundantly. Another brother from England who was in the islands at that time joined him. The name of this English man eludes me while I write this. The meetings were held in a large tent that had to be extended many times because of the increasing numbers that attended. The meetings continued for many weeks and the hand of the Lord was seen in the salvation of many. It was a time of revival. When the gospel effort concluded, the converts numbered well over fifty. Now another brother took over. He was a doctor and was exercised that these converts should be cared for. So he rose to the task. The work was not over with the preaching of the gospel - the sheep then needed shepherding. This brother gathered the converts in a hall that belongs to his family, or perhaps some other place. These gatherings of the converts and others led to the planting of the Ebenezer assembly. A few years later the Ebenezer Hall on Crompton Street was built and it has remained to this day. This is the large hall that I spoke in on my first visit to Barbados with Sally McCune. I remember that a brother named Robin Blair from Ballymena direction accompanied me for part of that trip. I missed Robin very much when he left Barbados for home after three weeks. He remembers the visit to this day and the names of the many people that he met at that time.

The conference lasted through Saturday all day and Sunday for the usual meetings. The hall was packed to capacity even in the gallery and many sat on chairs outside the windows all around the building. Many believers came from the United States and Canada and some from other islands in the Caribbean.

Some of the folk from the States and Canada were Barbadian born but had emigrated to the States and elsewhere. One of the speakers also came from New York and we became firm friends. Later he invited me to visit the assemblies in New York and I said that there was only one assembly in New York and it no longer existed. He informed me that there were eleven black assemblies in that large city. On my visit there I got round most of these meetings. We had a wonderful time in the conference, such a happy day with beautiful singing and searching ministry. I met many and made close friendships with some whom I later met again on my visit to New York.

An amusing thing happened at that time that Robin likes to talk about. Following the conference, the assembly in Fairfield had the brother from New York and myself for a night of ministry. All of us had our supper with Maggie and then we set out for the meeting. Sally took Betsy and Maggie in her car while Robin and I were in the car belonging to Maggie which she had lent to us during our stay. Sally led the way for we had no idea where the hall in Fairfield was situated. Sally raced ahead and we failed to keep up with her. She did not wait for us to catch up. Her eye was not on the mirror to see whether we were following. Maybe she was busy talking! We came to traffic lights and Sally drove on through the red light as it changed. We had to stop, then we moved on with the green light and Sally was gone.

We came to a junction but were without the knowledge of which direction Sally had taken. We decided to turn left, which of course turned out to be wrong. We ended up somewhere in the middle of Bridgetown, totally lost. We stopped and enquired of many where Fairfield was and none could answer. Then a young man informed us that he knew. He got in with us and directed us up and down streets until we came to a large hall, a very big Pentecostal church! By this time the meeting would have started. In fact, the New York brother spoke first and continued past his allotted time because I failed to turn up. Brethren in cars were out looking for us. At last I said to Robin, "We are near the coast now and we would be better to head for home". I knew that where Nell lived was on the coast. The meeting by this time would have been long over. Just as we arrived at Nell's home, a car came into the drive. It was Franklin Brown and his wife. Both were highly amused at our adventure in Bridgetown rather than being at the meeting. With smiling faces they informed us that everyone was still in the hall although the meeting was over. Everyone wanted to know what happened to us. We followed Franklin to Fairfield Hall and many were standing outside. They all cheered us as we arrived; the sisters laughed and said they thought that brother Jennings had driven into the sea. The dear brother from New York told us he preached till he could preach no more. The poor brother was exhausted.

Brethren were still coming in their cars to tell that they failed to find us. All were glad we had arrived, although too late for the meeting. Some of the sisters said that the next time I spoke I had to take twice the time for missing this meeting. Sally McCune was very much embarrassed and said she never noticed we were not following her. All was soon forgotten. We had a wonderful time with Robin, but after three weeks he had to leave us and catch up with his work at home. We missed him very much for the rest of that trip.

Now I must come to the close of the information about Barbados. Nell got married!

Nell was well known by most of the important people on the island of Barbados. Her family were among the aristocrats over many years. She was friendly with a number of very important people that visited Barbados from time to time. Among her visiting friends was a world-known concert pianist. This lady's name I fail to remember. However, this grand pianist was booked for a few nights for classical concerts in Bridgetown during one of my visits. Nell invited her for supper at that time and got a few folk in to hear the good lady play. Now the piano in the house of Nell was as ancient as the house itself. This instrument had not been tuned for years and many of the keys were stiff and some stuck when played and had to be lifted up again with a finger. At that time I tried to play a few hymns on it and gave up. It was a waste of time. I wondered how this talented pianist would cope with this old instrument. Well, the day arrived and the piano lady also arrived and a few other folk were present. The visiting pianist started with a few of Chopin's nocturnes. How she could play on such a piano amazed me. Her fingers just ran up and down that old piano with amazing speed. Notes stuck all over the place but she with tremendous speed slipped a finger under each one and did so with a speed that one could hardly notice. A most amazing woman! At one stage one of the notes flew into the air and fell on the floor. Someone lifted it up and handed it to the pianist. She just stuck it in and continued playing. At the end of the performance the husband of Nell shouted, "She can play almost as good as me!" This is the husband I wish to write about now.

Alf was an Irish man who came from the Limavady direction and he was a Christian. He was married and had at least one son. Alf's wife had died sometime before the things I write about. The son of Alf was trained as a cook and they came for a holiday to Barbados. The son desired to open a restaurant on the island. Later they found that this was impossible. The government did not allow outsiders to start such a business - that was the privilege of the locals. Alf just happened to stay with Nell as she kept guests at that time. When Alf saw the palatial house and this very mannerly Christian lady, he got very interested. He came back for another visit to Barbados and joined Nell in the assembly at Dayrells Road. He proposed to her and after some thought Nell agreed to get married to Alf. Soon Alf knew that Nell had little or no money and lived by keeping a few guests. However, that seemed to make no difference to Alf. He was a very likeable man. Alf and Nell were so different that I thought that the marriage would not last. Alf was a good few years older than Nell. He had worked as a prison officer and a bus driver over the years and retired when he came first to the Barbados. Nell never worked in her life and was used to servants for all the duties of a household. Alf was a very good handyman and was so useful in the large house that needed so many minor repairs to almost every room. He built cupboards in the kitchen; he was able to cook a lot better and faster than Nell. Also he could drive a car and purchased one and drove Nell all over the place to do her shopping etc. Nell made good use of this, one can imagine. When Alf appeared on the scene, things changed dramatically. Breakfast was on the table in a few minutes; dinners were on time and well cooked. A contrast to Nell who spent hours preparing a simple meal. The place was swept so clean every day. Before the Alf days, the place was covered in dust, meals were up to two hours behind time and many other such things. Alf brought a new atmosphere into the house. He was short in stature but in many ways he was a giant of a man.

However, Nell and Alf were so different from each other. Nell was so slow and just took her time with every task: Alf was smart and got all things done in a short time. Alf had humour and Nell did not know the meaning of fun. Unfortunately, Alf poked fun at Nell most of the time. Nell did not understand this and thought Alf was being unkind. Going to the meeting was always a problem. Alf was ready in very good time but Nell was slow and the time passed by without her knowing. Again she was always late, yes, and very late for every meeting. I did not want to be late as I was the speaker, so I made arrangements for some of the brethren to collect me. That was before the brethren arranged a car for me on later visits. At one time, Nell began to wonder if she had made a mistake in marrying Alf. This occupied her mind for a long time. During that time she asked me to help her with what the Scripture would teach in her situation. I borrowed a car and took Nell out of the house. Sitting in the car under a tree for shade I talked to her for about two hours and eventually she concluded that she loved him. I told her that it was obvious to me that she loved him. I also pointed out that she would miss him if he was not there. He kept the place going and he drove her in the car everywhere she had to go. Life had greatly changed for the better since Alf had come into her life. I remember an instant that occurred which is typical of how they had differences.

The garden at the back of the house was very extensive and often monkeys had to be chased away from the trees. This was difficult because the monkeys just ignored any one shouting at them. Monkeys thought they owned the place! This time it was not monkeys but a cat. Now Nell loved cats and Alf had little time for them. The trouble this time took place at tea time. A large cat was howling very loudly quite near the back door of the house. We failed to hear the conversation round the table for the roaring of the cat. Alf rose from his chair and said, "I am going to fix that cat once for all!" After a minute, the howling of the cat ceased. Alf came in and said he had thrown a stone at the cat. The stone had hit it between its ugly eyes. Nell was appalled This was a crime to her, and she began to preach to Alf that he would have to give an account of this wicked deed before the Judgment Seat of Christ. Alf winked at me. He had just thrown a stone and the cat had run away. He knew that if he said he hit the cat, Nell would be so annoyed - and this was a great joke to him.

At one time Alf thought it would be good for Nell to see Ireland, so they made a trip for a month or so to the Emerald Isle. This was in the summer time but Nell was so cold. She shivered the entire trip through, spending most of her time sitting against a radiator and taking several blankets to bed with her. Nell was born into the heat of the West Indies and the heat was part of her life. We had both of them in our home for a visit or two and Nell just sat shivering. Nell could never have lived in our country.

I must stop for a while writing about Nell and write of the presence of monkeys in Barbados. This came about some time in the past. The government decided to make a study of monkeys for some reason. They built a large compound with very large cages that contained quite a lot of monkeys. One night one smart monkey managed to tear a hole in the roof of one of the cages and leapt out to freedom and the other monkeys followed. They managed to open the other cages and all the monkeys escaped. It was impossible to round them up again, so the monkeys increased abundantly on the island. They think they own the place and cross the country roads with their little monkey children hand in hand. They glare at the drivers of cars if the traffic does not stop to let them cross over the road. Nell had visits from the monkeys every day in her large garden.

In latter times, Nell could not afford to keep the large house going. Guests now were going to apartments and the house was given over to a nephew of Nell. There was a little apartment built onto the side of the house that a brother of Nell built for himself. He had passed on and Nell lived in the little one bedroom apartment. Alf found this very restricting and so left for Ireland for a time. During that time, Alf stayed with Nell for a few months and then left for Ireland and England for a time. Nell refused to go with him because of the cold. Nell then passed away. I was so sorry to hear this and my wife took the news very badly for a long time. I never met anyone like Nell in all my life, so godly, innocent and different. There was only one Nell. Alf died a few years later. They were a couple who crossed my life and I could never forget them. I often feel that I would have missed something in life if I had never met Nell and Alf.

I have now come to the conclusion of my times in Barbados. I made about nine or ten trips in all and each trip brought new experiences to me. Most of the dear black brethren and sisters that I loved with all my being are now gone to be with Christ in the glory. There are still twelve assemblies functioning in Barbados and the work goes on. If the Christians are as spiritual as those in the past, all will be very well indeed. Sally McCune got to the age she could no longer live in the islands and retired to Faith House in Belfast. I used to visit her and when she was a hundred years of age she could still remember the names of all the beloved saints of Dominica. She wrote to them continually. Her writing at her age was neat and the lines so straight. Sally died when she was 102 and her works do follow her. She lived for the Lord and His work, especially in Dominica.

Port of Spain

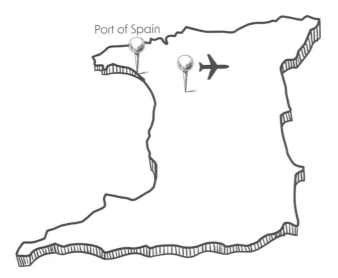

TRINIDAD

I never had any desire or exercise to visit Trinidad with the gospel. However, in a peculiar way the door opened to allow me to visit this large island and to try and help the assemblies there. This all came through a brother from Trinidad called Learie Telesford. First let me make a few remarks about this important island in the Caribbean.

The area of Trinidad is about 1864 square miles; one could put Barbados into this large area many times. The population when I was there was well over a million people, among them many Hindus that likely came from India sometime in the past. People of other races were very common and they all seemed to get on very well together. The one thing I did not like was the funerals of the Indian folk as they burned the bodies on the beaches of the island. The people of Trinidad were rather prosperous; this was largely because of the asphalt lakes that contained millions of tons of asphalt. I saw many large trucks coming from the lakes in great number and taking this substance that would end up on other islands. This was used for making roads in Trinidad and elsewhere. I noted that the roads were much better that those of the other islands I had visited. Dominica could do with loads of the asphalt! A lot of people lived in very good houses and excellent shops could be found all over the Island. The capital city was called Port of Spain which is a well-known city with excellent modern buildings. Just a ten minute flight takes one to Tobago, a lovely little island that is part of Trinidad.

As far as I could gather, assembly work commenced well over a hundred years ago. The first breaking of bread was in the year 1910 with just a few believers. About five years later a good hall was built and the numbers grew and this became known as Belmont Gospel Hall. Over the years the work developed with the help of missionaries from the homeland and elsewhere. One man in particular that left his mark was Henry Spencer with his wife Hettie and their two daughters. He was a very godly man, an earnest preacher of the gospel and he was used of the Lord to see many saved through the power of the gospel. This man laboured faithfully and planted at least two assemblies which are there to this day.

At the time I visited there were two missionaries working on the island, a brother from Scotland and Danny Ussher and his wife Audrey from Northern Ireland. Unfortunately, both of these men were on furlough when I happened to be in Trinidad. I was informed by the believers that there were twenty-six assemblies in Trinidad and five in Tobago.

Now to get back to the circumstances that led me to visit Trinidad for a little over four weeks.

Brother Learie Telesford came from Trinidad and worked with an oil company for many years on another island and then took early retirement. He was then commended to the work of the Lord by the assemblies on Trinidad. He had a wonderful interest in the gospel. Would there were many others that had such a keen interest in souls that they might get saved! Learie did some ministry as well, but his interest was in the gospel. Now this dear brother visited Dominica when I was there and we became firm friends. Another time when I was in Barbados, we shared a conference together. We were able to work in harmony and this was a blessing to the believers. One day when we were drinking coffee in one of the houses of the saints, he suggested that I pay a visit to Trinidad. I was not too interested, but he insisted we could have good times together in his home island. I then began to be exercised to do as he said and, taking it to be the mind of God, we made arrangements that I would take time off from Barbados and visit Trinidad. Now Learie got it into his head that I needed a rest. I was overworked with all the meetings I took in Barbados, so he thought. I arrived in Trinidad, was met by Learie and taken to his home. He lived in a very good and roomy house. His wife was called Lystra, a most encouraging woman, a great help meet indeed to Learie. That evening I preached the gospel in the open air with Learie and another brother. This meeting was held on a piece of waste ground with some houses a good way off. The next night again we did the same, preached on the waste ground. I thought it a waste of time as well as waste ground! In the morning, Learie took me to speak to the children in the schools. One morning I spoke in two schools and another two in the afternoon. In some of these schools the number of children was about a hundred. Others were very large schools and the young people at times were several hundred. In one school there were up to nine hundred listening to me. Most of the schools were open to the gospel and Learie took advantage of this. All this was good, but I came to help with the Word in some of the assemblies and the time was passing by. When I spoke of this to Learie, he said that I needed a rest from ministry. I thought then that my visit to Trinidad was going to consist of open air preaching and speaking in schools. However, I felt others on the island were dedicated to these works and I thought the need would be for a little teaching. That always goes a long way to help in assembly testimony. Now the two daughters of Henry Spencer had carried on with the work after their parents had passed on to be with the Lord.

It came to the ears of the two daughters of Henry Spencer that I was on the island. I never found out which was the elder of the two, whether it was Anne or Lillian, I think this was the name of the other. Anne was well known as she had travelled about quite a lot and had been in Northern Ireland a few times. She was well known in sisters' meetings, a lot more that the other sister. They knew of me, of course, because of their Irish visits.

When they heard I was with Learie preaching in the open air each evening to a few people and sometimes none it would seem, they came to fetch me to their home. Learie did not want me to go, but they insisted. I just sat there and let them come to some agreement. Lillian was a great talker. When she spoke, it was difficult to get a word in anywhere. Anne was most determined, so the two sisters won the day. Learie said he would keep in touch with me and maybe organise a trip to Tobago as he had a son living there. So the two girls took me to their home. It was a nice modern bungalow and they had meetings arranged for me in no time. In fact, they had booked me for a ministry meeting that very night.

Now both of these ladies were somewhat overweight. Some folk described them as "the rolly pollies". They knew of this, of course, but they did not mind. They were both hardy ladies who did a great work and sought to carry on where their father had left off. Anne and Lillian ran a school with a few hundred children enlisted and they made sure the gospel was preached to these little ones every day. They also were aware of the need for teaching and encouragement among the assemblies.

I remember the first meeting that night. I do not remember the name of the hall; suffice to say it was a very large building and that night it was filled from back to front with eager believers hungry for the Word of the Lord. I took up a passage from the Old Testament as far as I remember and many of the young folk especially were busy taking notes. I saw immediately that the Christians of Trinidad were serious in their faith and were seeking to go forward. After the meeting, many asked questions and I thanked the Lord for this. The next night, I had another meeting. Again it was a large hall and every seat was taken. Some dear ones had to stand throughout the meeting. I revelled in this keen interest in the Word. Learie also with his wife came to these meetings. He spoke in the open air somewhat earlier so as to be able to attend the meetings. When it came to Lord's Day, I was invited to four halls. I visited one and remembered the Lord with them and afterward ministered the Word. Then I was taken by some brethren to another assembly and again remembered the Lord and spoke the Word. I had never experienced this before, remembering the Lord twice on the same day. Now whether some believers think this ought not to be so did not matter to them or me. In fact, the next Lord's Day I remembered the Lord in three assemblies and spoke after the bread in these three places. That first Lord's Day, after the breaking of bread I spoke the Word in one hall in the afternoon and another in the evening. Learie and Lystra attended all these meetings. When I spoke to him, he always reminded me that I needed a rest! One evening they had me with the two Spencer girls for a meal before the meeting. Lystra told me that the ministry was very instructive and asked me many questions. I perceived that Lystra was a most intelligent believer; she had a tremendous interest in the Scriptures. I found this with many of the saints as I got to know them during that time in Trinidad. I was so sorry that Danny Ussher was away during this time. I would have loved to have had his cheerful companionship, but, alas, he was in Northern Ireland on furlough. A few months later we met at a conference in Northern Ireland and he told me he would have been delighted to have been in Trinidad when I was there. "Maybe sometime in the future we might be together in Trinidad", he told me, but that day never came. I got too old to travel and Danny passed on to be with the Lord.

There are about twenty-six assemblies on the large island and I managed to get to about twelve during that visit. I found the assemblies to be much in harmony with each other, with good leadership and an excellent interest in the Word. I would have liked to conduct a few Bible Readings at that time, but the saints were more interested in ministry. Again I had only one night or Lord's Day in each hall, so could not carry on a series on some neglected parts of Scripture or on the great subjects of typology or prophecy. A number of the saints asked me to stay for a few weeks longer or to return soon. At that time it was impossible to stay. I was to return to Barbados for a few days then journey home to Northern Ireland.

Some of the brethren and the two Spencer sisters took me to interesting parts of the island and I found it all so different to Dominica and Barbados in many ways. Everything was more modern and there was a great mixture of races. Many large buildings lined the beaches; posh hotels and many other things. No doubt, they went in for tourism like the other islands but commerce and business seemed to be the main source of income.

One experience I will not forget, and that is living in the same house as the Spencer girls. They were happy and so easy to get on with. They both loved the Lord and sought to serve Him to the limits of their power. They knew every assembly in Trinidad and I might say every individual in the assemblies as well. The need was great, especially for teaching, and the girls were well aware of this. From the day I entered their home I was booked for ministry meetings every night until the day I left.

They booked me in meetings where they thought the need for teaching was greatest. I soon saw that they were right in their choice of places to speak the Word. Young men were hungering for some helpful Bible teaching. It was clear that they would listen to the Word every night and I was willing to teach it. However, I had only a few weeks left. Because of just one night's ministry in each place, I did not get to know the believers personally as I did in Dominica and Barbados. There were quite a number that followed me from hall to hall and I was beginning to know them more personally but, alas, I had to leave them all so soon. On the whole the visit turned out to be very successful with the hand of God evident in the midst. Now if a desire for the Word was left in the hearts of the believers, then I was pleased and it was so.

As for Anne and Lillian, they were a delight to be with and most humorous at times. They were both great talkers, although Anne's words were about a third of Lillian's. They both used many words to describe something that could have been said in a few words. One sat at the end of the table at mealtime and the other sat at the other end. One talked and the other was waiting to spring in and to take over the conversation. Both struggled to get in all the time. I failed to get speaking, only a word shot in here and there. This reminded me of the time I used to preach in Northern Ireland with a preacher called Eric Wishart. He was a very joyful man howbeit a most serious preacher of the gospel with a deep love for sinners. He was a soul winner one could say but at times he could be very funny. We both were at the house of two little sisters for tea before a gospel meeting and were in the same situation as with the Spencer sisters. The two little ladies talked and talked and neither Eric nor I could get a word in edgeways. Eric then shouted, "Stop, stop, what we need at this table is traffic lights". I thought of this with the two charming sisters in Trinidad. Lillian spoke the most and one time after she had gone on for over a half hour, Anne said to her, "You speak too much! Sam wants to get his thoughts together for the meeting". However, Lillian just proceeded on and on.

Both had good appetites which would explain the extra weight they carried. During the time I stayed with the Spencers, I was able to do little jobs for them about the house. Their home was a delightful bungalow, but little things needed to be done all about the place. They were not good at simple repairs. They just paid the local tradesmen to do any little jobs and they did little or in some cases nothing at all and charged them abnormal prices. Now this brings me to the garden hose. The water just dropped within about two feet from the nozzle. Good pressure was missing. They got some workmen to deal with this problem. They did something to the hose that often made it worse and then charged dearly for the task. I saw that the hose just needed a washer and I went to a shop, purchased one that cost a few cents, put it on and, lo, we had a magnificent powerful hose that reached the far end of the garden. So I watered the garden every day for the two good ladies. Now they had a pet dog which was desperately overfed and overweight. The poor dog could hardly walk. It just looked like a large balloon or ball with four little sticks at the four corners and a little stick for a tail. The dog took to me for some reason and sat at my feet when we were at our meals at the table. A strong odour arose from the dog even at a distance. How much more at my feet when I was eating! I thought I would give the dog a wash with the strong hose. The silly dog followed me everywhere, even into the garden, but when the dog saw the hose in my hand, it refused to leave the kitchen. It just peeped at me from behind the door. I sat the hose down and called for the dog, but, no, it refused to come. Then I sat the hose behind the garage, intending to get it quickly and hose the dog, but it was too wise. After I had watered the garden and put away the hose in the garage and locked the door, the dog was prepared to come out and sit at my feet in the garden. I tried every trick I knew but the dog was too wise for me. I never got washing that dog. It remained the smelly dog at my feet until the last day I left Trinidad.

The time came when I left Trinidad with its streaming crowds of people: West Indian folk with many from India and a few Carib Indians. Not too many of these people can be found in the West Indies. The islands were first populated by tribes of Arawaks. They were peaceable and worked the land and lived an easy quiet life. The time came when the Carib Indians who lived on the mainland of South America invaded the island and slaughtered the Arawaks. Caribs were fierce and delighted in war. They were also good seamen and able to travel in long canoes across the very fierce sea. By the time Columbus came to the islands, the population consisted more of Carib Indians that any others. When the Spaniards came to the island, they almost wiped out the Carib Indians with the guns against the spear and bow. In Dominica, the natives fled into the thick forests and up the mountains. The Spaniards could not find them. To this day, there is a Carib reserve in a section of the island where they keep themselves to themselves and look upon visitors as unwelcome. When I was in Dominica, I paid a visit to this reserve. The brethren have sought to reach them with the gospel, but with no success as of yet, as far as I know.

To me Trinidad was a very large island. I really saw very little of it in the time I was there. Crowds of people seemed to fill the streets of the cities and in one way I was glad to get back to the more easygoing Barbados and Dominica.

During my adventures with the Bible in Trinidad, I will ever remember the school that was started and run by the Spencer sisters. This school began many years earlier when the girls were quite young. The school had increased in numbers over time so further teachers were required. This need was met by Christian teachers, some from the assemblies and others from Christian churches on the island. I was taken round the school by Anne; she gave me a most interesting tour. This first time it was late morning when the little children had a siesta time. They all lay on the floor of the large recreation hall, sound asleep. Each child had a little pillow under its head and a sheet for a bed. Not one was awake as far as I could see. The school started quite early and after a few hours of learning they had their siesta. After this they were refreshed and enabled to take in another hour or so of instruction. The children were so adorable and I was sorry afterwards that I did not take a photo of them all happy and sound asleep. I had the privilege of speaking to them at one stage to give the religious instruction they had each morning. The children all listened with great attention as I took up a Bible story. I went over the story in plain words then sought to learn one great lesson from that particular Bible portion. I asked a few questions afterward and all the answers proved that they had got the main lesson of the story in their little minds.

From what I know, that school was later taken over by the government as the two sisters in advanced years found it getting beyond them. A long time after my visit, the two Spencer girls came home to England and lived in a home for the aged. I never saw them again. They were two wonderful ladies who were missed when they finally left Trinidad after many years of service to the Lord and love for the people of the Lord. One could repeat the well-known truth that God buries His servants and carries on His work. Both Anne and Lillian shall without doubt hear the words from the Savour Himself, "Well done, good and faithful servants, enter into the joy of the Lord".

So I left Trinidad, sort of knowing I would never be back. I will always remember Trinidad, not because of the many things that appeal to the tourist, rather the dear believers and especially the two lovable Spencer girls.

10 GRENADA

On one of my preaching trips to Barbados a certain young girl asked me whether I would consider a visit to Grenada. I took this lightly not knowing the girl. I asked one of the brethren about her and was informed she came from Grenada and had found work in Barbados. I was also told that she belonged to another assembly in the city of Bridgetown. On another visit to Barbados, this same girl approached me and wanted to know if I could work in a visit to Grenada. Later she came and told me that her father had sent me word through her that I was to come to Grenada. I later learned that her father was one of the principal men in the assemblies of Grenada. I sent this man word that I would go at that time before I got all booked up for meetings in Barbados. He sent me word to book my flight and said they would reimburse me when I arrived. I made all the arrangements and after a few days I was on a flight from Barbados to Grenada, for I took this to be the mind of the Lord.

Grenada at one time was under the rule of Britain, as was the case with many of the islands of the Caribbean, but had received independence before the time I visited the island. The population of Grenada was at that time about 110,000 people. The area of the island is about half the size of Dominica. The length is about thirteen miles and the breadth about eight miles. However, the population was much greater than Dominica. Both Grenada and Dominica were quite mountainous with heavy growth of bushes and trees everywhere. Grenada is called the spice island and indeed it is. When I was there the first thing that a visitor like myself noticed was the heavy scent every morning on awaking from sleep. This was the scent of nutmeg, cinnamon and other such spices. The capital of Grenada is St. George's and the houses were very colourful. There were many old buildings that speak of the past history. I found that the climate was quite pleasant and the people very friendly. There had been some missionaries labouring there in the past, but at that time there were none, not even any on furlough. However, a good solid work had been accomplished and there were seven assemblies there at the time of my visit.

The later history of Grenada was very sad and terrible for most of the inhabitants. The island got independence from Britain in 1975 and there was a coup about five years later when the communists took over. It would seem that this all came from the influence of Cuba. Quite a number of people were killed during that time. The communist leader who sought to take over was a man called Maurice Bishop. He ended up in prison but was set at liberty again. Later on he died in the struggle. The communists were more or less in power until 1983 when America invaded Grenada. This was at the time Ronald Reagan was president of the United States. I heard varied stories about that time. However, the island woke up one morning to see many ships a mile or so off shore. There were one aircraft carrier, a few destroyers and other vessels. The landing crafts approaching the shore were filled with American soldiers. Most of the army recruits in the island were overawed when they saw all this in the early morning sunshine. Many of the Grenadian soldiers cast their guns into the water and into the bushes, took off their uniforms and hid them under trees and bushes, and fled home in their underwear. A few sought to fight, but it was all over in a day. Fewer than forty were killed in all. That was the end of the communist power on the island. When I was there everyone seemed to be content under the government that then existed. Grenada is now known as the State of Grenada. Most of the other islands were divided into parishes like the parish of St. Joseph or St. Michael and so forth. This is not the case in Grenada as far as I know. It is just known as the State of Grenada.

The little plane I travelled in landed at the airport in Grenada. The father of the girl that I spoke of was there to meet me. I cannot remember his name. I ought to have taken notes at the time and during the other trips I made to the U.S.A., Canada, Australia, Egypt and other places. I never dreamt I would one day write about the trips to West Indies and so need to keep a record of names. I remember some, but I met so many beloved saints that my mind cannot recall their names. I sort of remember that the name of this dear man began with W. West or Woust or something like it. I took to this dear brother and we became firm friends in no time. He with his wife and daughter lived in a nice comfortable house. I noticed they all had excellent teeth as is the case with most of the islanders. However, the folk of this house cleaned their teeth after every meal, especially the girl who was about 18-20 years old. She seemed to clean her teeth not only after every meal but times between as well. I must say she had wonderful teeth and she was a very nice girl in every way. She talked much about her sister in Barbados; they seemed to be very close sisters. The mother was good chat and did everything she could to make my stay a happy one.

I arrived quite early and the brother W. showed me around his local area. I saw an old fort that had been built hundreds of years earlier. The British were stationed there for many years. The fort was just loaded with history. I thought to myself that I must go and see that old building during my stay on this island. I saw other wonderful places of interest that had endured many years. As the hours went by, the raindrops started to fall and it turned out to be a very wet night. Now one thing I had learnt in my trips to the Caribbean islands was that the natives of each island had one thing in common: they did not like to get wet with the rain.

The reason for this is very obvious: the body is warm with the constant heat and the rain coming down from the heavens is extremely cold. This resulted in very severe colds and coughs and many other things. The first night the company was quite small. This was the first time I preached to a small number in all my travels in the West Indies. I had got quite used to a hundred and much more in every meeting so far. That is with the exception of some assemblies in little remote villages in Dominica. Being new to Grenada, I thought this was the usual number, that assemblies were small in size. It came to my mind that during a week of ministry in Dominica the numbers were most encouraging. However, the fourth night had turned out to be a wet evening. The dear saints came in open trucks packed in and all had large plastic bags over their heads and bodies. They had cut out circles for their faces. Some just cut large holes for their eyes and they looked like a bunch of aliens from another planet. I remember Sally McCune laughing her head off. She had actually never seen the like of that during all her years in Dominica. The believers were so interested in the Scriptures that they were determined to attend, rain or no rain. I thought that either the believers in Grenada did not think of plastic bags in place of coats and hats, or else the assemblies were small. No remarks were passed about the rainy night and a tall stately man opened the meeting before I spoke. This man was a lawyer and very highly trained and his name was brother Sylvester. In opening the meeting he stood up and proudly said, "We are greatly privileged to have with us tonight the greatest Bible teacher in this perishing world". I looked all round to see if some brother from Scotland had come in, maybe Jack Hunter or Albert Leckie. I did not think they could be possibly referring to me. By that time I had paid visits for Bible ministry about seven times to the islands and I always stayed for at least six weeks. Because I sought to just to open the Word in a sort of instructive way, I now had a reputation of being a Bible expositor, but I laughed into myself, "The greatest in the world! Wait till my wife hears this!" Anyway, as far as I remember, I took the meeting and sought to give an outline of the eight men of Genesis: Adam, Abel, Enoch, Noah, Abraham, Isaac, Jacob and Joseph.

Now an interesting thing happened while I was speaking that first night. I had just finished my reading and lifted up my eyes to the company about to talk and the lights went out. We were in total darkness. I began to speak as I did not need notes that first night. After a few minutes, a brother came up to the pulpit carrying a hurricane lamp and set it beside me on the platform, just about a foot from my Bible. Now this helped me to see my Bible, but it did something else as well. It attracted a swarm of insects to the light and they circled round and round the light and around my head as well. There must have been a hundred species of insects, some small and other quite large. There were many cockroaches. As I wrote earlier in this book, the cockroaches are very large in the West Indies and I found they were even much larger in Grenada. Also they fly in sort of long leaps when it is raining. This was a very wet night and the cockroaches were in great form, jumping up all over the place and around my head. Two of these sticky creatures landed on my Bible. I tried to swipe them away but to no avail. So I said, "Excuse me while I shake the roaches off my Bible". I then lifted my Bible and gave it a mighty shake over the side of the platform and continued to preach. The creatures were flying around me like something in a circus and I wondered if I would be able to continue. I was thinking to myself that I would be better without the lamp, when suddenly the lights came on again. The flying creatures soon disappeared and I was able to finish the meeting in peace. After the meeting not one mentioned this to me. It seemed to be a common occurrence with the lights in that section of Grenada.

I was booked for four nights in this particular hall. At supper time after the meeting the brother W. and his wife continued to ask me for more information about the subject I took up in the meeting. It was quite late when I went to bed, my first night in

Grenada. Now the following night was wonderfully different. It was a nice warm calm evening without any rain and the hall was packed to capacity. Many of the saints had feared to come out the previous night as it was so wet. Now, the next evening, the numbers were so great that many could not get into the hall, even to stand never mind sit. As all the windows and doors were open, the folk just sat on the grass banks around the hall and all were able to listen to the Word of the Lord. This interest continued to the closing night and I had to stand and answer questions from many young believers for a long time after each meeting. Again in the home each night it was quite late for bedtime. The family had to have the question time. How enjoyable!

During that first series of meetings, I had a few interesting experiences. The first was a visit to the old fort. I just walked to the fort seeing it was just over a mile from where I was staying. As I entered I was dressed in a pair of light trousers and a tee shirt as it was quite warm in the morning. As far as I could see, there was only one person in that old fort and that was a policeman. This man in uniform was sitting on a chair propped against the wall near the entrance. He knew I was a foreigner and asked me where I came from. I told him I was from Ireland and he asked me if I was in the I.R.A.. At that time the troubles were very severe in Northern Ireland. I answered this policeman telling him I was in no such organisation. He did not believe me and again spoke to me and asked me if I was there to bomb the fort.

I said, "Of course not! I am just interested in seeing over the old fort". He began to look all round me in search of bombs. I said, "Look, I have no parcels with me or a bag of any kind. Look, I am dressed in light tropical clothing". This was not good enough for this silly policeman. He followed me all round the old fort. He was just about three feet from me, dogging my steps. When I stopped, he stopped; when I moved, he moved. I thought of Israel in the wilderness, stopping when the cloud stopped and moving when the cloud moved. I am sure the policeman breathed a sigh of relief when I left the fort. Here I was in little Grenada in the Atlantic Ocean and they knew about the troubles in our little Northern Ireland. I was highly amused at the whole business. I did not know what would happen if a few robbers came to carry away one of the large cannons which weighed somewhat over a ton. This man guarding the fort had neither a gun nor a stick. I hope the folk that guarded the fort hundreds of years ago were better armed than this man!

Another thing I remember in Grenada was the ants. I encountered ants in all the islands I had been on so far, but Grenada triumphed over them all as far as the ant world goes. I looked at some trees in the garden of the brother I stayed with. I came close to one tree and it was swarming with ants all over the trunk. However, they moved very quickly in lovely order. One column was going up the tree and another column was coming down. Not one ant turned to go in the opposite way; it just looked like the M1 Motorway in England or the M1 in Northern Ireland. I then looked at another tree and it was the same. I found these ants everywhere. Maybe it was the season or the weather affecting them but at that time it was impossible to avoid them. The country places in Barbados were nearly like this, but Grenada won the day. I studied them very closely; they worked in harmony, a number of them would accomplish the same task. On looking to them I thought of the Scripture, "Go to the ant, thou sluggard, consider her ways".

The second day after breakfast and after we all had cleaned our teeth, the man of the house asked me if I was able to swim. I told him I could swim indeed. So he took me to a lovely beach that looked to be many miles long. Such a beach I had never seen - and just a few people in swim suits enjoying the sun. The powers that be at that time did not value this wonderful stretch of sand. At the edge near the road they had dumped all the rubble from houses that were being knocked down to give way to modern property. The sight of all these old broken bricks and cement with a large quantity of old rotten wood was an eyesore for anyone using the beach. A number of people were out swimming as the water was most calm and some were sunbathing, but there seemed so few of them considering the length of the lovely beach. Everybody just occupied the beginning of the beach that was closely adjacent to the town. Brother W. brought me to a nice little nook that he knew about and we had a swim. He thought himself a good swimmer and so he was. He pointed out a little rock off the shore. "Could you swim as far as that rock?", he asked. I told him I could. He said, "I will race you to the rock". Now I did not have many talents as far as sport was concerned. I never went in for football, as millions of people do, but I was a good swimmer. We both dived into the calm warm water and I swam ahead of him and was sitting on the rock when he arrived. He was amazed and asked me where I learnt to swim like that. I informed him that in early days I worked in bakeries making bread and every afternoon I went to the public swimming pools. In the summer I rode a bike almost every day to Helen's Bay in County Down and had a swim. All the time I was with this dear brother we had an early swim in the morning. I went for a walk every afternoon and had a visit to a few trees and plants to consider the ants. Such harmony and wisdom! I thought it would be wonderful if humans behaved like those little ants. Brother W. and I spent the evenings after the meetings talking about the good Word of the Lord. He was very well read and a spiritual man. We delighted in each other's company very much.

The meetings continued for the four nights and each evening there was present a man who was different from everybody else. This was because of his hair. He had long bushy hair that stood straight up in the air. It was all over his head like a big hairy cushion and it was as white as snow. He looked funny at first, but later I found he was a most delightful man and full of character. My next meeting was in a hall called Corinth. I thought that these must be rare brethren! I hoped they had some of the excellent gifts of the Corinthians without all their errors. This black man with the white bushy hair came and collected me. I was to stay with him for the few days of the meetings. The day came when I had to depart from the family, brother W. and his dear wife and the teeth-cleaning daughter. However, I was to return after the meetings in Corinth.

This dear brother drove an old van that had seen better days, yet it accomplished tasks that I never dreamed it could do. The road to his home was dotted with steep hills. Each hill seemed to be steeper that the one before. The little van kept going. The bushy brother then stopped to give some young people a lift as they do in the West Indies. Now with this larger load the little van went on. We came to a terribly steep hill that was very long as well. It seemed we were climbing a mountain road. I said to the brother that the van could never drive up this hill. He laughed and said, "Just you wait and see". The engine strained slower and slower until we almost came to a standstill. The young people jumped out of the van which made the load much lighter, but they all also began to push the van up the hill. During the task they were all laughing and broke out into song. Actually, it was a most interesting experience. We finally came to his home which was a sort of country cottage. I was shown a nice bedroom and a bathroom that would do me fine. Outside he had a marvellous garden that seemed to produce every vegetable and fruit one could imagine. He had a few animals and birds in cages about the place as well. One of these was a monkey in a fair-sized cage. This was the funniest monkey I ever saw. When you came near the cage, it gave a great demonstration of its abilities to jump and get into funny shapes. It would hang upside down and make a tremendous noise that would frighten one to despair if it was not all so amusing. "One must watch the keys of a car", the brother told me. "If they are in your hand, he grabs them so fast you could not see it. He can see also if they are in your pocket and he quickly thrusts his hand in and snatches them away. He then taunts you, putting the keys outside the cage and snapping them away when you try to catch them. He finally ends his show by throwing your car keys into the bush and it will take hours or days to find them".

Each morning I was awakened with a very loud rattle. I discovered it was the monkey running his tin food dish across the bars of the cage. This was him telling us it was time to get up and that he was hungry. Every day I had a session or two with the monkey and he showed me new tricks and laughed when he performed them. To tell the truth, I missed that monkey when I left the house after the meetings had finished. Much later when I attended the Easter conference in Belfast the brethren asked me to give a report on Grenada. At that time there was a scarcity of missionaries at home on furlough, so they turned to me. In my address I spoke of the monkey in the garden of the home of the dear man with the bushy hair. The people thought the monkey story was very amusing and many thought the story of the monkey was the best of the conference that year!

The meetings for the three or four nights in Corinth were well attended. One had to come quite early to get a seat and lots of people had to stand within and without the hall. One dear brother who had lately joined the fellowship of the assembly came from the Pentecostals. He was present every night and came early to get a seat at the back of the hall. All during the time I was speaking, he shouted with a voice like thunder, "Amen, Praise the Lord". I found that I had to speak much louder to be heard, then his "Amens" increased in volume also. The young sisters and others thought this was quite a joke. They had no experience of Pentecostal meetings on the islands, and they can be quite noisy indeed. I spoke about this to the brethren after the meeting. They informed me that he behaved like that in every meeting. They were afraid to approach him in case they offended him and he would leave the company. I thought I had better do something about this if the meetings were to be profitable to the believers. The second night I came early and the dear brother was already seated at the back of the hall. I sat down beside him. I asked him whether he enjoyed the ministry and he answered, "I certainly do". I asked him how he could listen when he was taken up with his own shouts of "Amen". He told me it was the Spirit of the Lord within him. I then asked him what the meeting was about the previous night and he had not a clue. I said, "The reason for this is that you are not listening to me but to yourself. The young people in the meeting are laughing to themselves". His "Amens" etc. were a source of amusement to them. I also told him that it was most difficult for me to speak with the terrible racket he made in his "Amens". I did all this as gently as I could. I also told him that I loved him and would be severely hurt if he left the meeting. Tears came to the eyes of the dear man. He asked me if he really made it difficult for me to speak. The dear brother was greatly disturbed at this. "I will try tonight to be quiet", he said with great emotion. I told him he could cry an "Amen" at the end of the meeting as the others did. I saw him leaning forward and his eyes glued upon me throughout the meeting and he only uttered one "Amen" when I was finished, as did others. When he was going out, he shook my hand and said, "How did I do?" "Wonderful", I said, "you are a good man". He then said to me, "I just love you, dear brother". I was deeply touched by this. For the rest of the nights the man was as quiet as a mouse and saved his "Amen" for the end of the meeting. The dear brethren of Corinth asked me how I accomplished this. I told them that it had been done by love to the man and by prayer.

Out of the seven assemblies, I had the time to spend three or four nights in four of them. The numbers were overflowing every night, except the first one, that rainy night when I was announced as the world-renowned Bible teacher!

I left the dear brother with the bushy hair and the monkey and returned to brother W. and his family and the teeth-cleaning lovely daughter. My final night was in that first assembly and brother Sylvester again opened the meeting and did so with tears. They all felt it keenly that this was my last night in Grenada. Many tears were shed that night, including my own. Of all the islands so far in my experience, Grenada was the one I would have been so pleased to go to if the Lord had called me there to continue His work in a more permanent way. Or, better still, I would just have loved to have been a missionary called to the work of the Lord in Grenada from the beginning. However, God's will, not mine, must be done.

ANGUILLA

had never heard of Anguilla until I came on my third visit to Barbados. While attending a meeting in which I was to speak with another brother, I first heard of Anguilla. We were talking about the wisdom of brother Fred Ashby when a brother said that he had a brother called William Ashby. William was commended by the assemblies of Barbados to the work of the Lord on the little island of Anguilla. A few days later, I was asked to Fred Ashby's for a meal. Now the wife of Fred had died a few years before I ever came to Barbados. Quite a few dear single sisters had their eye on Fred, hoping to become the next Mrs. Ashby. To the amazement of all, Fred made a trip to Canada and came home with a new wife. This good Christian lady won her way into the hearts of all the saints of Dayrells Road assembly and further afield. In no time, she was the most popular sister on the island. My wife became a friend of Mrs. Ashby and they were very close. Quite a few times we were invited to their home for a meal, which was always very sumptuous. So on this occasion while at the table I mentioned brother William and asked about him. Fred told me he was a very fine brother who had got saved and had been in fellowship in Dayrells Road assembly for quite a few years. He had a keen interest in the gospel and then the Lord called him to go to Anguilla to forward the gospel in that little island. I thought no more about this. On a later visit, I got a phone call from William Ashby from Anguilla inviting me to come to the island for a week or two. He had heard of me and thought the small assembly would profit from the ministry the Lord gave me.

I found it impossible to go at that time but promised to go later in the will of the Lord.

I never gave much thought to the conversation until during a later visit. William phoned me again. I told him that I was going to Dominica for three weeks and I would fly from there to Anguilla when I had finished my time in Dominica. After two weeks I went to the LIAT office to purchase my ticket to Anguilla. As there were no direct flights to Anguilla, I had to travel via Antigua, change planes there, then on to Anguilla. I remember the time I bought the ticket. Generally, the girls in the LIAT office are very efficient, but this was not the case with the girl in the office in Dominica. The ticket came to 396 dollars and I handed her 400 dollars. She took out a calculator and subtracted 396 from 400 and then gave me four dollars change. I asked her if she could have done this without a calculator. She looked at me and said, "But that is what calculators are for". I was told to come in on Tuesday to confirm the flight. I was to depart on Saturday, so I called the next day to confirm the flight. I was told to come and do so on Wednesday. I did so and was told to come on Thursday then Friday to confirm the flight. My flight was never confirmed. In fact, they could get me to Antigua but it would be Wednesday before I could get a flight from there to Anguilla. The way these companies operated was to heavily overbook the flights and before the time there would be quite a few cancellations, and all would be well. It was not so for my flight. It was anything but well. The flight from Antigua to Anguilla was completely overbooked by about 20 people - and the plane had a seating capacity for twenty people. There was no room for poor brother Jennings!

I prayed about this and thought I would cancel the whole arrangements and just stay in Dominica. There was plenty of work there. Then I thought I would go as far as Antigua and work something out afterward.

This I did and the plane arrived quite early in Antigua. Dalmar Edwards met me and took me to his home.

We both thought it better to inform William Ashby by phone that I could not get a flight until Wednesday. This I did. William was very annoyed as I was booked to speak on the radio in the afternoon and to take a meeting on Saturday evening and every night until Friday. I told him it was not possible. I was down the list to twenty other folk that were booked before me. Then he said, "Do nothing, let me pray about this". I told Dalmar and he then told me, "William is a wonderful man of prayer. Let be and see what the Lord will do". So we waited.

I told Dalmar that I likely would be staying with him for a few days. He said, "Wait and see". We drank coffee and talked for about half an hour. The phone then rang ... William Ashby was on the phone. He told me that after getting into the presence of the Lord, he was assured there was a seat on the plane for me.

"Go quickly, the plane takes off very soon", was all he said. Dalmar took me to the airport in the old battered car, the same one he had when I met him at first. Eventually we arrived at the crowded airport. I went straight to the check-in point for Anguilla and was alarmed to see a line of about thirty people. Now my plane was due to leave in fifteen minutes, so I just went to the front of the line, apologising to each person in the line as I passed. All were exceptionally nice. When I got to the counter I just put my ticket on the desk and the attendant immediately said, "Mr. Jennings, you are at the top of the list of passengers. Here is your ticket, and just carry your luggage to Gate 6". I hurried to Gate 6 and went onto the tarmac. The little plane was there with the props already going. The pilot standing outside the aircraft, looking at his watch. As I approached, he asked, "Are you Mr. Jennings?" I affirmed that I was. "Jump in", he said as he took my baggage and threw it into the back of the plane. He shut the door, got in to the little plane and flew off. I sat in amazement at all this. The change, from the bottom of the list to the top, how did this happen? I glorified the Lord in my heart. God had done the impossible. My name had risen from the bottom to the top of the list of passengers. I looked forward to meeting brother Ashby.

The flight took about an hour and landed at Anguilla. A black man approached me to greet me, introducing himself as Willie Ashby. His first words to me were, "I knew you were on that plane because the Lord never yet has disappointed me in anything I have prayed for". I beheld and considered this man of faith and prayer. In appearance he looked thin and somewhat bent over. It turned out he had a slight deficiency in his spine. He took my bag and led me to an old Datsun Sunny car, now called a Nissan. The car had numerous dents in the body work and the stuffing of the seats was sticking out in quite a few places. He took me to a very neat Gospel hall with a very good apartment attached to the back. I met his wife, quite a charming lady. He also had a little black girl that lived with them. Apparently she was homeless and was taken in by these two very spiritual believers.

I had the use of a lovely cute bedroom. The apartment was not very large but exceedingly comfortable. In the corner of the lounge stood a lovely black piano. I asked who in the house played the piano and was informed by William that his good wife was a music teacher. She had quite a few pupils and this helped in the upkeep of the household.

I must make a few remarks on the little island of Anguilla.

The island is almost 12 miles in length and about 3 miles in breadth. The island is called in Spanish –"Anguilla", which is the word for eel. The island is long just like an eel. Anguilla was under the rule of many nations in the old days like most of the islands in the Caribbean. The British got control and from the year 1650 it became a British colony. For a long time it was ruled by St. Kitts, a neighbouring island, but later was able to bring about its own rule. Anguilla has no particular town; the whole island is just like a scattered village, a little cluster of homes here and there with many solitary homes dotting the land also.

The weather is beautiful and there are plenty of beaches to enjoy all along the coasts. Most of the other islands are divided into parishes, not so with Anguilla; some of the districts are called after a sort of ground after the idea of the parables of the sower. The hall was in Stony Ground. The next to it was Sandy Ground and there were some other grounds, I suppose. There were other districts as well. I was not long enough on the island to get to know all the places and districts. The population at the time I was there was a little over six thousand. As far as I know, this has doubled to twelve thousand or more. At the time of my visit, there was very little in the way of hotels. Now there are quite a number around the coasts of the island. When I was there, there was a sort of exclusive camp that was cut off from the outside with strong fences. It was a sort of health camp for the very well-to-do folk from North America. I heard that it was dreadfully expensive to stay there and most people stayed for several months at a time. I only saw the place from the outside so I have no idea what the accommodation was like; it must have been very grand to suit the rich clientele that made use of it.

The address of the Gospel Hall was in Stony Ground. This was the only assembly on the island and there were about twelve in fellowship. Many other people attended the hall who were saved but not in the fellowship as yet. They had the usual breaking of bread meeting and a gospel meeting on a Lord's Day and a prayer and teaching meeting during the week. I was there for meetings from Saturday night to the following Friday and then I had to leave for other places.

My first day in Anguilla was to first enjoy a lovely meal prepared by Mrs. Ashby and the little black girl who lived with them. In the afternoon I was booked to speak on the local radio at 3 p.m. Some may question speaking on the radio, but this was set up and it would have been upsetting to some if I had refused to do the job. The man who interviewed me was quite talkative. He asked me why I had made this visit to Anguilla. I told him that I had come to let the folk know what the Bible was all about. He asked me to give my testimony and I spoke of my experience of getting saved through the death of the Lord Jesus upon the cross. He then questioned me about my call to the work and I spoke of this also. I managed to get the gospel into most of what I talked about. This interview lasting about half an hour was heard all over the island. This resulted in excellent crowds at every meeting. After coming home and enjoying another meal, we went to invite people to the meeting that evening. We used his little Datsun car and went round the district. Most people were working in their gardens and everyone knew brother William. Everyone was smiling. They were such a happy people. The young girls were all busy working and wearing old garments to do the gardening work, especially the growing of fruit trees and vegetables. We must have called to about fifty homes and we were very tired when we got back to the house. After a little rest it was time for the first meeting.

Now with only twelve in fellowship I expected a small number of people, but I was delighted to see many people, in some cases whole families. Brother William was out collecting people in a lovely carrier bus that could seat about twenty or more. He made several trips and each time the bus arrived another twenty or more people came into the hall. When it was time for the meeting to begin, the hall was filled to capacity. All I could see from the platform was a crowd of happy faces of both young and older people. I ministered the Word for a while for the believers, and then preached the gospel for the other half of the meeting. What a joy it was to speak to so many happy and eager people. Every night was the same, right to the final Friday night. The hall was packed to capacity with many standing outside. I followed the same idea, first the ministry followed by the gospel as many unsaved were present in the meetings.

After the meeting each night we had a cup of tea together and the wife of William give us a recital on the piano. She played a number of hymns with variations and ended up with some classical pieces from Beethoven and Chopin and others. It was always a restful and delightful evening and made one ready for bed. After the first meeting in the evening while we partook of our supper, I asked about the lovely van that was used for the meeting. William informed me that it was a gift from the black assemblies of New York; they even paid the carriage for the van right to the door of the hall. I knew without asking that all this had been an answer to prayer.

On one of these nights after the meeting I passed a remark about the nice hall and apartment. William told me that all of it was the Lord's answer to prayer. Then he told me this story.

When he had the exercise to live and to preach the gospel in Anguilla, there was nothing to start with. He rented a little house and rented a public hall for meetings. After some labour, a few people were reached and saved and William was exercised about the building of a hall. He had very little money so he used what he had to purchase a plot of ground to build on. He then had no money left. He prayed that the Lord would provide the money for the building of a hall. He prayed for some time very much about this, but the Lord did not send any money. Then one day a builder called to see him and said that he was building some houses. The firm in St. Kitts had sent too many bricks and blocks. He did not want to spend the money sending them back: could he use them? William put the bricks in his lot that he had purchased. A few days later another builder called and asked him if he ever thought of building a hall. William then received without cost enough window frames complete with the glass for nothing. The same happened with timber. A building project was oversupplied and the builder wanted to get rid of the surplus timber. The same happened with toilets and tiles even electric wiring with dozens of plugs and all. This went on for several weeks and William discovered he had enough to build both a hall and an apartment. The site was large enough for this, with space left for a car park. Now he could build a hall, but who was to build it and where was the money to pay the workers? William made this a matter of prayer. As he prayed, the Lord brought before him a certain builder who had a business in St. Kitts. He was in an assembly there. He decided to pay him a visit and did so. He arrived at the brother's home at lunch time, having taken a short flight from Anguilla. The wife of the builder told him her husband was out inspecting the building projects he had in hand. William was invited to wait and join them for dinner. The brother came home and was delighted to see William. William had decided not to say anything about the hall that needed to be built. However, during the meal the builder brother suddenly said, "Did you ever think of building a hall in Anguilla?" William then told him he had all the materials to build one. The brother then told him that he would build the hall. He told William that the Lord had blessed him and that if ever there was to be a hall in Anguilla, he would build it without charge. All he asked was that William would provide meals for his workers. As for accommodation, he would put his crew up in a small hotel. Within a year both the hall and the apartment were standing on that plot of land that William bought. The whole matter of a hall was provided by the Lord without asking anybody for anything. I was thrilled at all this. I had never met a man of such faith and prayer before this. I was very moved. This little bent over man was a giant for God. He reminded me of the great cloud of witnesses of Hebrews 11, men of faith, and of the Lord in Chapter 12.

William and I had a swim every morning. The first time he took me in the battered Datsun to a lovely shore where about six people were scattered over the long beach. William said that this beach was too crowded. He took me to another shore. This consisted of soft sand with the waves gently rolling in. A boat needing repaired was hauled up to the grass that ran alongside the beach and there we changed and had our daily swim.

I also went shopping with my host. The shop was about three miles from the hall and home. One day the little battered Datsun refused to start. I said that we could take the van. He said, "Oh no!", and explained that the van was given for the work of the Lord and not for the use of personal journeys. Therefore, we had to walk. Now to walk a total of three miles to the shop and three miles back was quite a task, especially on the homeward journey as we were carrying bags of goods with the narrow grips biting into our hands. I was quite fit at the time and with a short rest after the task I was recovered. I was amazed at the energy of William. He did not look fit but he was as fit as a fiddle, one would say.

About halfway through my stay in Anguilla, someone told me that the doctor surgeon on the island was an Irish man from Belfast. I thought I would go and see this Belfast man. I went to the little hospital and was surprised to see such a neat building and right up to date. I enquired of the doctor to a receptionist and she told me the doctor was in the surgery, cleaning up the operation room after an operation. I could just go in and speak to him. How different from the hospitals that I know of in the homeland. I had to remember that this was the West Indies where everything is more easy going and this was a very small island where all the people knew of each other. I went into a perfect surgery, the scene of an operation just a few hours before I arrived. The handsome doctor was busy cleaning the place and asked me what he could do for me. I said that I had just called to see another Irishman. When he heard my accent, he was delighted. We had a wonderful chat together. He had been sent to the island for a period of four years and was halfway though this time. His wife just loved the island and was quite prepared to stay if the way opened up. He felt differently and thought he would not like to spend his working life in such a small world. However, he liked the people and the peace that existed plus the nice warm and healthy climate that prevailed. He was from the countryside in Northern Ireland but had trained in Belfast and lived there before his assignment to Anguilla. This came about because Anguilla was a British colony. I intended to pay another visit to him, but was too busy and the time too short to do so.

The little perfect hospital was of the best that money could buy and wonderfully efficient. I thought of the hospital in Dominica which consisted of a few tin army huts and a few nurses and flies everywhere. The beds did not look very clean and there were a few patients lolling about. I felt that that hospital could make one more ill than staying at home.

Sunday School, Anguilla

A Sunday school was carried on in the Gospel Hall the whole year round. The attendance was around the thirty mark. I spoke at the school on the Lord's Day I was with the saints. The little children were ever so adorable. I took a picture of some of the pretty children smiling as always. I got to know the little company of believers very well. The few brethren were outnumbered by the sisters, but they all were so loving and helpful. I just loved that little Anguilla Island and the Lord's dear beloved people. It was such a very happy and blessed week I had with William, his wife and the saints that I will never forget. He told me to come back the next time I visited the islands, but I found this impossible to do so. I know that if he prayed that I would return, the Lord would have opened the way to do so.

Brother William died about three years ago and believers came from many of the other islands to attend his funeral. He was very well known in most of the other islands and brother Lionel Weeks had the honour of speaking at his funeral. I would have loved to have been there. William Ashby was renowned for his prayer life. He had many experiences of answered prayer in impossible situations that glorified God and met the need of many. I was deeply affected by this dear man. To him the Lord was everything and his confidence in God's power and grace had a great effect on all who knew him.

In conclusion, the visits to the Island of the Caribbean and the dear beloved saints I met made a difference in my life before the Lord. The happy and spiritual believers impressed me very much. I saw Christian love in operation as it should be and rejoiced in the tremendous hunger to know the Scriptures. I can only say, "The Lord is Good".

At this present time, there are a few from North America who work in the West Indies, but none from Scotland, England, nor from the Emerald Isle. All of the small islands are without missionaries.